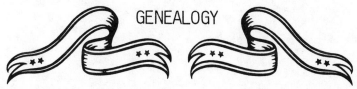

A Basic Research Guide for Tracing Your
Civil War Ancestors with Detailed Sources
and Precise Instructions for Obtaining
Information from Them

by

George K. Schweitzer, Ph.D., Sc.D.
407 Regent Court
Knoxville, TN 37923

Typed by

Anne M. Smalley

TABLE OF CONTENTS

Chapter 1

THE CIVIL WAR

1. Introduction

From 12 April 1861 until 26 May 1865 there raged
what has come to be called the Civil War (War Between the
States, War of the Rebellion, War of Secession, War for
Southern Independence). On one side were eleven Southern
states organized as the Confederate States of America
(CSA, Confederates, the South, Rebels or Rebs), and on
the other were the remaining states of the United States
of America (USA, Union, the Federals, the North, Yankees
or Yanks). About 1,500,000 fought for the Union with
about 1,000,000 for the Confederacy. Many of the battles
were exceptionally bloody with enormous casualties. At
least 270,000 were killed in battle, over 440,000 died
from illness and other causes, and about 500,000 were
non-fatally wounded. Since the population of the US in
1861 was approximately 32,000,000 this means that over 7%
(one out of every 14) of the people were directly involved. Anyone, therefore, who had ancestors who were
living in the US in 1861, has a high likelihood of being
the descendant of one or more Civil War veterans. Of the
large volume of records kept by both sides, many have
survived and are very fruitful sources of genealogical
information.

2. The background

In the decade 1851-61, a number of differences between the northern and southern states were intensifying.
Involved were the issue of slavery with its economic,
social, legal, and moral implications, the issue of the
relations between the southern agrarianism and the grow-
ing northern industrialism, and the issue of federal
control against states' rights. Compromises which had
worked well early in the decade and before failed in-
creasingly and violent conflict loomed over the US in the
early months of 1861. By 04 February 1861 seven southern
states had seceded from the Union (SC, MS, FL, AL, GA,
LA, TX). On this date they met, set up the Confederate
States of America, adopted a constitution, and elected
officials. On 12 April 1861, Confederate forces began to
bombard the Federal Fort Sumter in the harbor of Charles-

ton, SC.   On 14 April 1861, it was surrendered. Lincoln
called for troops to be used against the seven southern
states, and by 24 May 1861 four more southern states had
joined the Confederacy (VA, AR, TN, NC).   This left the
following states in the Union: CA, CT, DE, DC, IL, IN,
IA, KS, KY, ME, MD, MA, MI, MN, MO, NV*, NH, NJ, NY, OH,
OR, PA, RI, VT, WV*, WI, the states with asterisks being
ones which were admitted to the Union during the War.
Both the Confederacy and the Union mobilized their man-
power and resources, and four years of tragic conflict
had begun.   A brief summary of the major events of the
War now follows.

3. Brief history

It was the intent of the Union to defeat the Confederate states by invasion and so to forcibly demon-
strate that their secessions were not valid. The history
of the Civil War can be seen as the fulfillment of five
strategies on the part of the Union:
1) the blockading or capture of southern ports to cut
   off supplies,
2) the taking of the Confederate capital Richmond by
   attack from the north,
3) the winning of control of the Mississippi, Tennessee, and Cumberland Rivers which would secure supply
   and transportation routes,
4) the splitting of the Confederacy by driving a wedge
   from northwest TN to southeast TN to Atlanta to the
   GA coast at Savannah, and
5) moving north from the GA coast into SC, then NC,
   then assaulting Richmond from the south at the same
   time the Confederate capital was being attacked from
   the north.

Strategy 1), the sea blockade of the Confederacy,
was accomplished early in the War with the blockades or
captures of most Atlantic Coast ports, the capture of New
Orleans, LA 28 April 1862, and the capture of Fort Pulas-
ki 12 December 1862 effectively closing the port at
Savannah, GA.

Strategy 2), the drive toward Richmond from the
north, included the Union defeat 21 July 1861 at First
Bull Run (a small VA stream 30 miles SW of Washington),

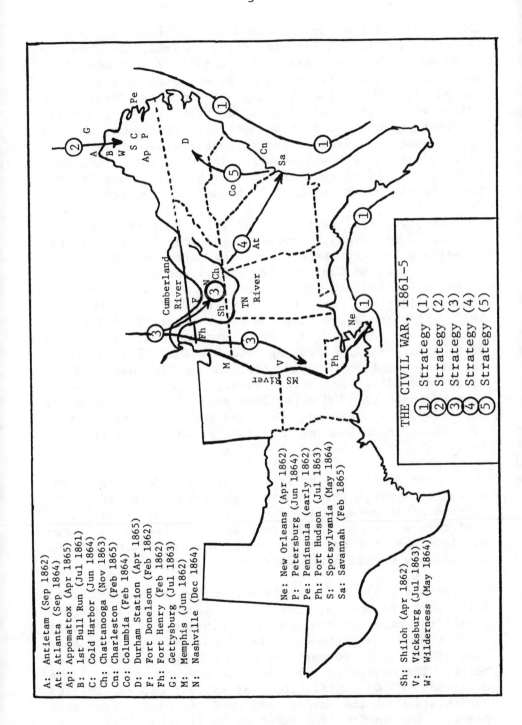

A: Antietam (Sep 1862)
At: Atlanta (Sep 1864)
Ap: Appomattox (Apr 1865)
B: 1st Bull Run (Jul 1861)
C: Cold Harbor (Jun 1864)
Ch: Chattanooga (Nov 1863)
Cn: Charleston (Feb 1865)
Co: Columbia (Feb 1864)
D: Durham Station (Apr 1865)
F: Fort Donelson (Feb 1862)
Fh: Fort Henry (Feb 1862)
G: Gettysburg (Jul 1863)
M: Memphis (Jun 1862)
N: Nashville (Dec 1864)

Ne: New Orleans (Apr 1862)
P: Petersburg (Jun 1864)
Pe: Peninsula (early 1862)
Ph: Port Hudson (Jul 1863)
S: Spotsylvania (May 1864)
Sa: Savannah (Feb 1865)

Sh: Shiloh (Apr 1862)
V: Vicksburg (Jul 1863)
W: Wilderness (May 1864)

THE CIVIL WAR, 1861–5

① Strategy (1)
② Strategy (2)
③ Strategy (3)
④ Strategy (4)
⑤ Strategy (5)

the failure of the Union campaign to come up the VA peninsula to get at Richmond early in 1862, the invasion of MD and PA by the Confederates until 17 September 1862 when their slow retreat began at Antietam (a creek near Sharpsburg, MD), the halting of another Confederate offensive on 01-04 July 1863 at Gettysburg, PA, the drive of Grant against Lee in four battles: Wilderness, VA (19 miles west of Fredericksburg) and Spotsylvania, VA (10 miles south of Fredericksburg) in May 1864, and Cold Harbor, VA (10 miles northeast of Richmond) and Petersburg, VA (22 miles south of Richmond) in June 1864.

Strategy 3), the taking of the chief river systems of the Confederacy, involved gaining control of the Cumberland and Tennessee Rivers by capturing Fort Henry (34 miles west of Clarksville, TN) on the Tennessee River 06 February 1862 and Fort Donelson (25 miles west of Clarksville, TN) on the Cumberland River 16 February 1862, effectively clearing the upper Mississippi River by winning at Shiloh, TN (100 miles west of Memphis) on 06-07 April 1862, capturing New Orleans 28 April 1862, capturing Memphis 06 June 1862, taking Vicksburg, MS (35 miles west of Jackson on the river) 04 July 1863, taking Port Hudson, LA (200 miles down river from Vicksburg) 09 July 1863, and capturing Chattanooga, TN in the battles of Lookout Mountain and Missionary Ridge 24-25 November 1863.

Strategy 4), the splitting of the Confederacy involved the march from Chattanooga south in May 1864, the capture of Atlanta 02 September 1864, the defeat of a Confederate attack in the rear at Nashville on 16 December 1864, and the taking of Savannah on 22 December 1864, effectively dividing the Confederacy in two.

Strategy 5), the simultaneous moves on Richmond from both south and north, involved a drive from Savannah north to take Charleston and Columbia, SC in February 1865, then a push into North Carolina, while at the same time other Union forces bore down upon Richmond from the north. The surrender of the Confederate force in VA occurred on 09 April 1865 at Appomattox, VA, and the capitulation of the other major Confederate army took place at Durham Station, NC on 26 April 1865. This ended the conflict except for two further surrenders, one of the Confederate forces in AL and MS on 04 May 1865 and a final one of the trans-Mississippi forces on 26 May 1865.

4. Records

This very long war generated vast quantities of records of various types, many of which have survived and are available for searching. These records include military plans, draft records, enlistment records, military unit rosters and reports, medical records, supply records, battle reports, prisoner-of-war records, burial records, military tribunal records, ship records, court martial records, pension applications, pension records, regimental histories, military maps, naval unit histories, individual diaries, officer biographies and lists, photographs, personal reminiscences, and many others. The records are chiefly in the National Archives in Washington, DC and in the various state archives. However, many records are also located in historical society libraries, museums, manuscript collections, university libraries, county courthouses, town halls, churches, and national and state memorials, monuments, and parks.

5. Recommended reading

The above account of the Civil War is merely a brief outline. It mentions only the major battles, many others being fought as the five major strategies were carried out. Should you want to do more detailed reading, it is recommended that you begin with two or three short treatments. Suitable materials for this include:

THE ENCYCLOPEDIA AMERICANA, Americana Corporation, New York, NY, Vol. 6, pp. 782-819.

B. A. Weisberger, consultant, FAMILY ENCYCLOPEDIA OF AMERICAN HISTORY, Reader's Digest Assn., Pleasantville, NY, 1975, pp. 221-7.

L. B. Ketz, editor, DICTIONARY OF AMERICAN HISTORY, Scribner's Sons, New York, NY, Vol. 2, pp. 61-9.

R. B. Morris, editor, ENCYCLOPEDIA OF AMERICAN HISTORY, Harper & Row, New York, NY, 1976, pp. 268-292.

L. Shores, editor, COLLIER'S ENCYCLOPEDIA, Macmillan, New York, NY, 1979, Vol. 6, pp. 516-55.

H. H. Kaglan, editor, THE AMERICAN HERITAGE PICTORIAL ATLAS OF US HISTORY, American Heritage, New York, NY, 1966, pp. 194-241.

__C. D. Linton, THE BICENTENNIAL ALMANAC, Nelson, New York, NY, 1975, pp. 158-190.
__M. B. Grosvenor, AMERICA'S HISTORYLANDS, National Geographic Book Service, Washington, DC, 1967, pp. 392-479.
__M. Matloff, AMERICAN MILITARY HISTORY, US Army, Washington, DC, 1973, pp. 184-280.

Following these short discussions, if you wish you may go further by delving into one or more of the better one-volumed treatments of the Civil War. Recommended are:
__R. M. Ketchum, THE AMERICAN HERITAGE PICTORIAL HISTORY OF THE CIVIL WAR, American Heritage, New York, NY, 1960.
__P. J. Parish, THE AMERICAN CIVIL WAR, Holmes & Meier, New York, NY, 1975.
__E. S. Miers, THE AMERICAN CIVIL WAR, Golden Press, New York, NY, 1961.
__J. F. Rhodes, HISTORY OF THE CIVIL WAR, Macmillan, New York, NY, 1917.
__B. Catton, THIS HALLOWED GROUND, Scribner's Sons, Garden City, NY, 1956.
__R. P. Jordan, THE CIVIL WAR, National Geographic Society, Washington, DC, 1969.

Should you care to go much deeper into Civil War history or portions of it, the best sets of volumes available are:
__B. Catton, THE CENTENNIAL HISTORY OF THE CIVIL WAR, Doubleday, Garden City, NY, 1965, 3 vols.
__A. Nevins, THE WAR FOR THE UNION, Scribner's Sons, New York, NY, 1959-71, 4 vols.
__S. Foote, THE CIVIL WAR, Random House, New York, NY, 1958, 3 vols.
Also to be recommended is a volume which summarizes each day's important military events for the entire period of the War:
__E. B. and B. Long, THE CIVIL WAR DAY BY DAY, Doubleday, Garden City, NY, 1971.

A very interesting, well-edited, and attractively-printed journal for Civil War history fans is published monthly. It is called THE CIVIL WAR TIMES ILLUSTRATED, and it carries articles, pictures, columns, book reviews, and advertisements relating to all aspects of the history of the Civil War. You may want to examine a copy in your local library with a view to subscribing. Or you may want to send $2 to the following address for a sample copy:

__CIVIL WAR TIMES ILLUSTRATED, Historical Times, Telegraph Press Bldg., Harrisburg, PA 17105.

In recent years, several large, slick-paper, picture-laden, coffee table volumes on the Civil War have been printed or reprinted. These books are usually quite expensive, but they often can be found on sale. They contain beautiful pictures, detailed maps, charts, tables, and illustrations accompanied by descriptive material. Among those you might want to look at are:

__H. S. Commager, ILLUSTRATED HISTORY OF THE CIVIL WAR, Promontory Press, New York, NY, 1976.

__THE CENTURY WAR BOOK, Arno Press, New York, NY, 1894 (reprint 1978).

__R. Johnson, CAMPFIRE AND BATTLEFIELD, Fairfax Press, New York, NY, 1894 (reprint 1978).

__F. Leslie, ILLUSTRATED HISTORY OF THE CIVIL WAR, Fairfax Press, New York, NY, 1895 (reprint 1977).

__J. S. Blay, THE CIVIL WAR, Bonanza Books, New York, NY, 1958.

As you might imagine, the literature on the history of the Civil War is utterly enormous. An extremely useful 2-volumed set of books lists many of the works and gives each of them a critical evaluation:

__A. Nevins, J. I. Robertson, and B. I. Wiley, editors, CIVIL WAR BOOKS: A CRITICAL BIBLIOGRAPHY, Louisiana State Univ. Press, Baton Rouge, LA, 1967-9, 2 vols.

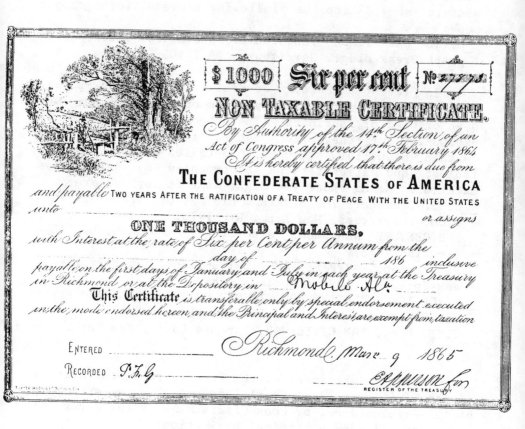

$1000 Six per cent No. 2~~~~

NON TAXABLE CERTIFICATE.

By Authority of the 14th Section of an Act of Congress approved 17th February 1864

It is hereby certified that there is due from

THE CONFEDERATE STATES OF AMERICA

and payable TWO YEARS AFTER THE RATIFICATION OF A TREATY OF PEACE WITH THE UNITED STATES

unto _____ or assigns

ONE THOUSAND DOLLARS,

with Interest at the rate of Six per Cent per Annum from the

day of _____ 186_ inclusive

payable on the first days of January and July in each year at the Treasury in Richmond or at the Depository in Mobile Ala.

This Certificate is transferable only by special endorsement executed in the mode endorsed hereon, and the Principal and Interest are exempt from taxation.

ENTERED _____ Richmond, Mar 9 1865

RECORDED P.F.G _____

_____
REGISTER OF THE TREASURY

Chapter 2

THE ARCHIVES

1. Basic information

In the Civil War, the vast majority of Union men served in the Volunteer Union Army. Considerably fewer served in the Regular Union Army, in the Regular Union Navy, in the Volunteer Union Navy, and in the Union Marines. Regulars were those men who were making the military their life's occupation. Volunteers were those who signed up only for the Civil War. Thus, if you had a Union Civil War ancestor, chances are high that he was in the Volunteer Union Army, but he could have served in the other branches. In the Confederate service, a man could serve in the Confederate Army, in the Confederate Navy, or in the Confederate Marines. If you had a Confederate Civil War ancestor, chances are he was in the Confederate Army, since the vast majority served in this branch, although much smaller numbers served in the other two branches.

The most easily accessible genealogical information on your Civil War ancestor will be found in the National Archives and in the archives of the various states which were involved in the conflict. It is helpful to know some basic things about your ancestor in order to have the professional searchers in the archives look for him: (1) his full name, (2) the state from which he entered military service, (3) whether he was Union or Confederate, (4) which branch of the service he was in, and (5) at least one other identifying characteristic (such as birth date, enlistment date, regiment, ship, whether wounded or killed or captured, wife's name). If you cannot now supply all this information, some guidelines for obtaining it will be given later.

2. National Archives

The National Archives is located on Pennsylvania Ave., between 7th and 9th Sts., NW, Washington, DC 20408. It is open 8:45 am-10:00 pm weekdays, 8:45 am-5:00 pm Saturdays, and is closed on Sundays. Their holdings include very large amounts of material on Union veterans plus considerable holdings on Confederate service men.

For UNION personnel the major Civil War records include draft records, service records, medical records, court-martial records, pension records, and burial records. For CONFEDERATE personnel usually only service records are available. In general, service records include such items as enlistment date, enlistment place, muster rolls, capture records, prisoner of war records, wounds, deaths, hospital notations, discharge place and date, promotions, and changes of military unit.

The major Civil War records which you should obtain for your ancestor are the service records and the pension records. To obtain the records for a Volunteer UNION soldier, you first need to know his, state, his regiment, and his company. You will usually know or can guess his state, and you can find his regiment and company in one of the following microfilm state indexes:

National Archives, MICROFILM INDEXES TO COMPILED SERVICE RECORDS FOR UNION ARMY VOLUNTEERS, 1861-5, M263 (AL), M532(AZ Terr), M383(AR), M533(CA), M534(CO Terr), M535(CT), M536(Dakota Terr), M537(DE), M538(DC), M264 (FL), M385(GA), M389(IL), M540(IN), M541(IA), M542 (KS), M386(KY), M387(LA), M543(ME), M388(MD), M544(MA), M545(MI), M546(MN), M389(MS), M390 (MO), M547(NE Terr), M548 (NV), M549 (NH), M550(NJ), M242(NM Terr), M551 (NY), M391(NC), M552(OH), M553(OR), M554(PA), M555 (RI), M392(TN), M393(TX), M556(UT Terr), M557(VT), M394(VA), M558(WA Terr), M507(WV), M559(WI), M589(US Colored Troops), M636(Reserve Corps), arranged in alphabetical order of name, gives branch of service, regiment, and company.

These microfilms (which are identified by numbers M263, M532, etc.) were produced by the National Archives, and copies have been purchased by many agencies. They are therefore available in the National Archives, in National Archives Field Branches (at or near Atlanta, Boston, Chicago, Denver, Fort Worth, Kansas City, Los Angeles, New York City, Philadephia, San Francisco, Seattle), in many large genealogical libraries, in the Family History Library in Salt Lake City, and in many state libraries or state archives. They may also be borrowed through the numerous Family History Centers (branches of the Family History Library), and by your local library or by you personally from AGLL, PO Box 244, Bountiful, UT 84010.

Once you know the state, regiment, and company of your Union ancestor, you can then proceed to get his service and pension records. The _service_ records for some states are obtainable on the following microfilms:
_National Archives, MICROFILM COPIES OF COMPILED SERVICE RECORDS FOR UNION ARMY VOLUNTEERS, 1861-5, M276(AL), M399(AR), M400(FL), M403(GA), M397(KY), M396(LA), M384 (MD), M404(MS), M405(MD), M427(NM Terr), M401(NC), M395 (TN), M402(TX), M692(UT Terr), M398(VA), M508(WV), M1017(US Volunteers), arranged by branch of service, then regiment, then alphabetically by name.
These microfilms are available in the same places mentioned in the above paragraph: National Archives, Field Branches, Family History Library (and its branch Family History Centers), large genealogical libraries, state libraries and/or archives, and from AGLL. The service records for all other states are available only in their original form in the National Archives. They must be ordered using Form-NATF which they will send you. Or, for faster service, you can hire a researcher in Washington, DC, to do the work for you.

Union _pension_ records are available only in their original form in the National Archives, where they reside in alphabetically-arranged files. To obtain copies, you must order them using a separate Form NATF-80. Or, for faster service, you can hire a searcher in Washington, DC. Pension records are likely to be exceptionally valuable genealogically. They may contain data for the veteran and his wife regarding places they lived after 1865, their marriage place and date, their birth dates and places, their children and children's ages, their death dates and places, plus other valuable items. Unfortunately, hardly ever will you find their parents' names.

To obtain the records for a CONFEDERATE soldier, you first need to know his state, his regiment, and his company. These data may be found in the following microfilm index which lists all Confederate soldiers for which the National Archives has records:
_National Archives, CONSOLIDATED MICROFILM INDEX TO COMPILED SERVICE RECORDS OF CONFEDERATE SOLDIERS, M253 (All Confederate states combined), arranged alphabetically by name, gives state, branch of service, regiment, company.

This microfilm is available from the several places
mentioned at the end of the second paragraph of this
section: National Archives, Field Branches, Family History Library (and its Branch Family History Centers),
large genealogical libraries, state libraries and/or
archives, and from the AGLL.

Once you know the state, regiment, and company of
your Confederate ancestor, you can then proceed to get
his service and pension records. The service records are
obtainable on the following microfilms:
__MICROFILM COPIES OF COMPILED SERVICE RECORDS FOR CON-
FEDERATE ARMY VOLUNTEERS, M311(AL), M318(AZ Terr),
M317(AR), M251(FL), M266(GA), M319(KY), M320(LA),
M321(MD), M269(MS), M322(MO), M270(NC), M267(SC),
M268(TN), M323(TX), M324(VA), M258(Confederate Government Units), M331(General & Staff Officers), arranged
by branch of service, then regiment, then alphabetically by name.
These microfilms are available from the several places
mentioned at the end of the second paragraph of this
section: National Archives, Field Branches, Family History Library (and its branch Family History Centers),
large genealogical libraries, state libraries and/or
archives, and from the AGLL.

Confederate pension records are available only from
the State Archives or State Library of those states which
gave pensions to their Confederate veterans and their
widows. These states are AL, AR, FL, GA, KY, LA, MS, MO,
NC, OK, SC, TN, TX, and VA. To obtain the pension materials, you must write the State Archives or Library in the
appropriate state. Send them an SASE (self-addressed
stamped envelope) and a $5 check with the payee line left
blank along with your request. Ask them to use the check
if there are charges, or if they cannot do the work, to
hand your the letter and check to a searcher who can.
Addresses for the state agencies to write are given in
the next section (section 3) of this chapter, and more
detail on Confederate pension lists is provided in section 4 of Chapter 4.

The above approach is one which will lead you to
most Union soldiers and most Confederate soldiers. The
large majority of men served in these roles, but there
were some other servicemen which will not be covered.

Therefore, if you know or suspect your ancestor served in the War, but you have not located him in the indexes listed above, you should seek him in some other records. In the event that your Civil War ancestor served in the Regular Union Army, the Union Navy, the Union Marines, the Confederate Navy, or the Confederate Marines, you will need to utilize other indexes. Your approach should follow the guidelines suggested in the following sections of this chapter: 8 (Regular Union Army), 9 (Union Navy), 10 (Union Marines), 11 (Confederate Navy and Marines). It is also possible that your ancestor served with a local militia unit or a local home guard unit for which few, if any, records were kept or whose records never reached the Federal or Confederate level. Such records should be sought in the pertinent state library and archives and at the local (county) level.

The vast Civil War resources of the National Archives, only some of which we have as yet discussed, are listed in detail in three major reference works. The first is more general than the last two which go into great detail and which have very useful indexes:

_National Archives Staff, GUIDE TO GENEALOGICAL RESEARCH IN THE NATIONAL ARCHIVES, National Archives and Records Service, Washington, DC, 1982.

_K. W. Munden and H. P. Beers, GUIDE TO FEDERAL ARCHIVES RELATING TO THE CIVIL WAR, National Archives Publication No. 63-1, General Services Administration, Washington, DC, 1963.

_H. P. Beers, GUIDE TO THE ARCHIVES OF THE GOVERNMENT OF THE CONFEDERATE STATES OF AMERICA, National Archives Publication No. 68-15, General Services Administration, Washington, DC, 1968.

All three of these volumes will be found in most medium to large size libraries.

Later in this chapter many more of the abundant resources of the National Archives will be called to your attention. These include records of pension payments, medical treatment, drafts, prisoners, hospitals, burials, wartime taxation, Provost Marshalls' activities, civilians, amnesty oaths, pardons, claims, and many others. However, before we go into these, we will discuss the State Archives, since it is absolutely essential that you contact them about your veteran.

3. State archives

After having looked into the holdings of the National Archives, the next step in your Civil War ancestor quest is to contact the archives of the state in which he enlisted. Even if the National Archives has provided you with extensive information, there is a good possibility that there will be more data available from the state archives. But, especially if the National Archives has not come up with anything on your ancestor, or if your ancestor was a Confederate, an inquiry to the state archives can be very productive.

Every state has archives where historical records are stored, indexed, and made available for research purposes. Some of these archives are extensive and well-staffed; others are under-funded and have difficulty in meeting all the demands made upon their personnel. However, without exception, these agencies do an excellent job in serving the needs of persons who request assistance. The state archives are especially useful if your veteran was Confederate since pensions were awarded to Confederates only by the individual states. Also the state archives are the only sources for men who were in the State Militias from various states. These militias were never directly attached to the Union or the Confederate government even though many of them served valiantly both within and outside their states.

To make an inquiry, send an SASE (self-addressed stamped envelope) and a check for $5 (with the payee line left blank) to the proper state archives. Ask them to look into their Civil War military service records and their Civil War pension records if a Confederate is involved. Send them as much information as you can: full name, enlistment date, enlistment place, home county, town, and/or city, age, etc. The addresses of the various state archives follow (Confederate states marked *):
__AL*: Military Records Division, Dept. of Archives and History, 624 Washington Ave., Montgomery, AL 36104.
__AR*: AR History Commission, 300 West Markham St., Little Rock, AR 72201.
__CA: CA State Archives, Archives Bldg., 1020 O Street, Sacramento, CA 95814.
__CO: Division of State Archives and Public Records, 1530 Sherman St., Denver, CO 80203.

CT: Records Officer, The Adjutant General's Office,
State Armory, 360 Broad St., Hartford, CT 06115. Also
CT Historical Society, 1 Elizabeth St., Hartford, CT
06115.

DE: Division of Historical and Cultural Affairs, Hall
of Records, Dover, DE 19901.

FL*: Dept. of State, Division of Archives, History, and
Management, The Capitol, Tallahassee, FL 32304.

GA*: Dept. of Archives and History, Civil War Records
Section, 330 Capitol Ave., SW, Atlanta, GA 30334.

IL: Director, Archives-Records Management Division,
Office of Secretary of State, Springfield, IL 62706.

IN: Archives and Records Management Division, Military
Records, Indiana State Library, 140 Senate Ave.,
Indianapolis, IN 46204.

IA: State Historical Dept., Division of Historical
Museum and Archives, East 12th and Grand Ave., Des
Moines, IA 50318.

KS: KS State Historical Society, 10th and Jackson Sts.,
Topeka, KS 66612.

KY: KY Division of Archives, 300 Coffee Tree Rd.,
Frankfort, KY 40602. Also KY Historical Society, Old
State House, Frankfort, KY 40601.

LA*: Director, LA State Archives and Records, Secretary
of State, PO Box 4422, Capitol Station, Baton Rouge, LA
70804.

ME: ME State Archives, State of ME, L-M-A Bldg., Augusta, ME 04330.

MD: Archivist, State of MD, Hall of Records, PO Box
828, Annapolis, MD 21401. Also MD Historical Society,
201 W. Monument St., Baltimore, MD 21201.

MA: War Records Section, Room 100, The Adjutant General's Office, Military Division, 100 Cambridge St.,
Boston, MA 02202.

MI: MI History Division, State Archives, 3405 North
Logan St., Lansing, MI 48918.

MN: Reference Services, Division of Archives and
Manuscripts, MN Historical Society, 1400 Mississippi
St., St. Paul, MN 55101.

MS*: Dept. of Archives and History, PO Box 571,
Jackson, MS 39205.

MO: Adjutant General's Office, 1717 Industrial Dr.,
Jefferson City, MO 65101.

NV: Secretary of State, Division of Archives, Capitol
Bldg., Carson City, NV 89701.

__NH: The Adjutant General, State Military Reservation, 1 Airport Rd., Concord, NH 03301. Also NH Historical Society, 50 Park St., Concord, NH 03301.

__NJ: Archives and History Bureau, New Jersey State Library, 185 West State St., Trenton, NJ 08625.

__NM: State Records Center and Archives, 404 Montezuma St., Santa Fe, NM 87501.

__NY: Bureau of War Records, Division of Military and Naval Affairs, Public Security Bldg., State Campus, Albany, NY 12226. Also NY State Library, Empire State Plaza, Albany, NY 12230.

__NC*: The Search Room, Archives Branch, Division of Archives and History, Dept. of Cultural Resources, 109 East Jones St., Raleigh, NC 27611.

__OH: Director, Division of Soldier's Claims (Veterans Affairs), Adjutant General's Department, State House Annex, Columbus, OH 43215. Also OH Historical Society, 1985 Velma Ave., Columbus, OH 43211.

__OK: Director, Research Library, OK Historical Society, Historical Bldg., Oklahoma City, OK 73105.

__PA: Director, PA Historical and Museum Commission, Archives Bldg., Box 1076, Harrisburg, PA 17108.

__RI: Adjutant General's Office, 1050 North Main St., Providence, RI 01903.

__SC*: SC Dept. of Archives and History, PO Box 11188, Capitol Station, 1430 Senate St., Columbia, SC 28211.

__SD: Historical Resources Center, Memorial Bldg., Pierre, SD 57501.

__TN*: Archives Section, TN State Library and Archives, 403 7th Ave., North, Nashville, TN 37319.

__TX*: Director of State Archives, TX State Library, Box 12927 Capitol Station, Austin, TX 78711.

__VT: Director, State Office of Veterans' Affairs, City Hall Bldg., Montpelier, VT 05602. Also VT Historical Society, PO Box 578, Wilmington, VT 05363.

__VA*: Archives Division, VA State Library, 12th and Capitol Sts., Richmond, VA 23219.

__WV: Dept. of Archives and History, Science and Cultural Center, Capitol Complex, 400 East State Capitol, Charleston, WV 25305.

__WI: Archives Division, The State Historical Society of WI, 816 State St., Madison, WI 53706.

Sometimes you will receive a reply from certain of the state archives indicating that they simply do not have the staff to do your work. In such a case, they can usually can supply a list of researchers who live nearby.

If they do not supply a list of such persons to you, researchers may be found in:

V. N. Chambers, editor, THE GENEALOGICAL HELPER, Everton Publishers, Logan, UT, latest Sep-Oct issue. This publication, a bimonthly journal, is the genealogical magazine with the largest circulation. It is available in practically all libraries which have genealogical holdings.

Several of the state archives mentioned in the previous paragraph issue guidebooks or pamphlets or leaflets describing their Civil War holdings. Write those you are interested in, send them an SASE, and inquire about costs of the guidebooks or pamphlets or leaflets. Hours when state archives are open, telephone numbers, and a listing of copying services in each are given in:

F. R. Levstik, DIRECTORY OF STATE ARCHIVES IN THE US, Society of American Archivists, Chicago, IL, 1980.

4. Detailed record information

In section 2 of this chapter, you were told how to easily obtain the _major_ information on your Civil War ancestor which the National Archives has among its large volume of records. This easy approach, as you will recall, is simply to use National Archives microfilms, and/or to order records from the Archives, or to hire a researcher to do the same work for you. However, it may be that you desire to do part or all of the work yourself, or you may wish to be able to direct the work of your hired researcher more effectively. It could also be that you wish to go beyond the _major_ Civil War records of genealogical value, and look into the vast volume of _subsidiary_ National Archives records which relate to the War. The remainder of this chapter will therefore be devoted to describing both the _major_ records (which we have all ready discussed) and many of the most-promising _subsidiary_ records which you might wish to dig into, if it is your desire to leave no stone unturned. You may be content with simply using the above microfims and letting the Archives or a hired researcher delve into the _major_ sources and if such is the case, you can skip the rest of this chapter, and go directly to the next chapter.

The extensive Civil War resources of the National Archives exist in two main forms. _First_, there are the original records themselves and a sizable number of card and manuscript indexes to them. These are available only in the National Archives. Second, there are microfilm copies of many of the more useful records and microfilm copies of indexes to them. These microfilms are available in the National Archives, and some of them are also available in the Regional Branches of the National Archives, the Family History Library of the Genealogical Society of UT in Salt Lake City, other large genealogical libraries, and state archives and/or libraries. Branches of the National Archives are located in or near Atlanta, Boston, Chicago, Denver, Fort Worth, Kansas City, Los Angeles, New York City, Philadelphia, San Francisco, and Seattle. They may be located by looking under FEDERAL ARCHIVES AND RECORDS CENTER in the telephone directories of these cities. There are also hundreds of branches of the Family History Library (called Family History Centers) through which their microfilms may be borrowed. They may be located by looking under CHURCHES-LATTER DAY SAINTS in the Yellow Pages of telephone directories in larger cities and towns.

Many of the major microfilms issued by the National Archives are also available from the American Genealogical Lending Library (AGLL), PO Box 244, Bountiful, UT 84010. These include indexes of Union service records for each of the states that had Union soldiers (see item 1 in section 6), compiled service records for Union soldiers in southern states (see item 2 in section 6), the consolidated index of service records for all Confederates (see item 1 in section 7), and the compiled service records for Confederate soldiers in southern states (see item 3 in section 7). These microfilms may be borrowed for you from AGLL by your local library, or you may borrow them yourself directly from AGLL. There is a small fee for each microfilm roll. This borrowing program permits you to check the Union service record indexes for your Union ancestor, to check the Confederate service record index for your Confederate progenitor, and to obtain the service records for both your Confederate and/or Union forebears who served on either side in a southern state. The use of these records can save you time and money because they will allow you to do some of the work that National Archives personnel would do (if you write them) or your hired researcher would do (if you hire one). You will still have to write them or hire a researcher for Union service records in the northern states and for union pensions, since these are not available on microfilm. In short, (1) all National Archive originals and microfilms will be found at the National Archives. (2) Some major microfilms and some subsidiary ones will be found at Genealogical Society of UT (GSU) and are available through Branches of the Genealogical Society of UT (GSU). (3) Some major microfilms are available at National Archives Branches, state libraries, state archives, and large and medium genealogical libraries, especially those microfilms pertaining to their regions. (4) Most major microfilms are available through AGLL. You may make use of these microfilms by several means (as mentioned above): mail, interlibrary loan (AGLL and Branches of the Genealogical Society of UT), personal loan (AGLL), hired researcher, personal visit.

In the sections to follow, both National Archives original records and indexes and also microfilm copies will be listed for the various military services. Remember that the original materials are only in the National Archives, so they must be examined there (by you, by a hired researcher, or by the Archives personnel). However, the microfilm copies are more broadly available and may be found in locations nearer you. All microfilm copies in the listings to follow will contain the word MICROFILM. If a listing does not contain this word, it refers to original materials available only in the National Archives.

5. Records for all Union forces

Among the more useful of the records available which cover all the Union forces are the following. These records apply to the Volunteer Union Army, the Regular Union Army, the Volunteer Union Navy, the Regular Union Navy, and the Union Marines.

National Archives, MICROFILM GENERAL INDEX TO PENSION FILES, 1861-1934, T288, arranged alphabetically by name, gives application, certificate, file numbers, state, and service data.

National Archives, PENSION FILES, 1861-1934, arranged by application, certificate, or file number.

National Archives, PENSION OFFICE FIELD RECORD BOOKS, 1805-1912, Record Group 15, record payments to pensioners, arranged alphabetically by name of city from which pension was administered (obtain from PENSION FILES).

There are no pension records in the National Archives for men who served in the Confederate forces, since the US did not award them pensions. The number T288 in the first entry is a microfilm identification number.

6. Records for the Volunteer Union Army

Please recall that the large majority of Union Civil War combatants served in the Volunteer Union Army. The records of military service in this branch of the armed forces include those listed below. You will notice that there are microfilm indexes for each state, but that the actual service records have been microfilmed for only some of the states.

__National Archives, MICROFILM INDEXES TO COMPILED SERVICE RECORDS FOR UNION ARMY VOLUNTEERS, 1861-5, M263 (AL), M532(AZ Terr), M383(AR), M533(CA), M534(CO Terr), M535(CT), M536(Dakota Terr), M537(DE), M538(DC), M264 (FL), M385(GA), M389(IL), M540(IN), M541(IA), M542 (KS), M386(KY), M387(LA), M543(ME), M388(MD), M544(MA), M545(MI), M546(MN), M389(MS), M390 (MO), M547(NE Terr), M548 (NV), M549 (NH), M550(NJ), M242(NM Terr), M551 (NY), M391(NC), M552(OH), M553(OR), M554(PA), M555 (RI), M392(TN), M393(TX), M556(UT Terr), M557(VT), M394(VA), M558(WA Terr), M507(WV), M559(WI), M589(US Colored Troops), M636(Reserve Corps), arranged in alphabetical order of name, gives branch of service, regiment, and company.

__National Archives, MICROFILM COPIES OF COMPILED SERVICE RECORDS FOR UNION ARMY VOLUNTEERS, 1861-5, M276(AL), M399(AR), M400(FL), M403(GA), M397(KY), M396(LA), M384 (MD), M404(MS), M405(MD), M427(NM Terr), M401(NC), M395 (TN), M402(TX), M692(UT Terr), M398(VA), M508(WV), M1017(US Volunteers), arranged by branch of service, then regiment, then alphabetically by name.

__National Archives, COMPILED SERVICE RECORDS FOR UNION ARMY VOLUNTEERS, 1861-5, arranged alphabetically by state, then branch of service, then regiment, then alphabetically by name.

__National Archives, ABSTRACTS OF MEDICAL RECORDS, 1861-5, arranged by state, then regiment, then approximately alphabetically by name.

__National Archives, MICROFILMED COPIES OF COMPILED

SERVICE HISTORIES OF VOLUNTEER UNITS OF THE UNION ARMY, 1861-5, M594, arranged by state, then regiment.
National Archives, CIVIL WAR DRAFT RECORDS: CONSOLI-DATED LISTS, Record Group 110, arranged by state, then by congressional district, then by age group and marital status, then alphabetical according to first letter of name.
National Archives, CIVIL WAR DRAFT RECORDS: DESCRIPTIVE LISTS, Record Group 110, arranged by state, then congressional district, then variously.
The numbers such as M263, M532, M383, and M692 are microfilm identification numbers.

7. Records for the Confederate Army

The large majority of Confederate Civil War participants served in the Confederate Army, only small numbers being members of the Confederate Navy or Marines. The records of military service in this army are listed below along with indexes. Unlike the Union case, there is an overall Confederate Army index which includes all the states from which Confederate soldiers fought. There are also separate state indexes. In addition, the service records for all Confederate states have been microfilmed.
National Archives, CONSOLIDATED MICROFILM INDEX TO COMPILED SERVICE RECORDS OF CONFEDERATE SOLDIERS, M253 (All Confederate states combined), arranged alphabetically by name, gives state, branch of service, regiment, company.
National Archives, MICROFILM INDEXES TO COMPILED SERVICE RECORDS OF CONFEDERATE ARMY VOLUNTEERS, M374(AL), M375(AZ Terr), M376(AR), M225(FL), M226(GA), M377(KY), M378(LA), M379(MD), M232(MS), M380(MO), M230(NC), M381(SC), M231(TN), M227(TX), M382(VA), M818(General & Staff Officers), arranged alphabetically by name, gives branch of service, regiment, company.
MICROFILM COPIES OF COMPILED SERVICE RECORDS FOR CONFEDERATE ARMY VOLUNTEERS, M311(AL), M318(AZ Terr), M317(AR), M251(FL), M266(GA), M319(KY), M320(LA), M321(MD), M269(MS), M322(MO), M270(NC), M267(SC), M268(TN), M323(TX), M324(VA), M258(Confederate Government Units), M331(General & Staff Officers), arranged by branch of service, then regiment, then alphabetically by name.

__National Archives, MICROFILM COPIES OF COMPILED SERVICE RECORDS OF CONFEDERATE SOLDIERS WHO SERVED IN ORGANIZA- TIONS RAISED DIRECTLY BY THE CONFEDERATE GOVERNMENT, M258, arranged by organization, then by company, then alphabetically by name.

__National Archives, MICROFILM COPIES OF COMPILED SERVICE RECORDS OF CONFEDERATE GENERAL AND STAFF OFFICERS AND NONREGIMENTAL ENLISTED MEN, M331, arranged alphabeti- cally by name.

__National Archives, MICROFILM COPIES OF UNFILED PAPERS AND SLIPS BELONGING IN CONFEDERATE COMPILED SERVICE RECORDS, M347, arranged alphabetically by name.

__National Archives, MICROFILM COPIES OF COMPILED RECORDS SHOWING SERVICE OF MILITARY UNITS IN CONFEDERATE ORGAN- IZATIONS, M861, arranged by state, then branch of ser- vice, then regiment or organization (including re- serves, militia, local defense, prison guards).

__National Archives, MICROFILM COPIES OF REGISTER OF CONFEDERATE SOLDIERS, SAILORS, & CITIZENS WHO DIED IN FEDERAL PRISONS AND MILITARY HOSPITALS IN THE NORTH M918, alphabetically by prison or hospital name, then alphabetically by surname.

__National Archives, MICROFILM COPIES OF SELECTED RECORDS OF THE WAR DEPARTMENT RELATING TO CONFEDERATE PRISON- ERS, M598.

__National Archives, MICROFILM COPIES OF INDEX TO LETTERS RECEIVED BY THE CONFEDERATE SECRETARY OF WAR, 1861-5, M409, arranged alphabetically by name; this index leads to microfilms of the letters.

__National Archives, MICROFILM COPIES OF INDEX TO LETTERS RECEIVED BY THE CONFEDERATE ADJUTANT GENERAL, INSPECTOR GENERAL, AND QUARTERMASTER GENERAL, M410, arranged al- phabetically by name; this index leads to microfilms of the letters.

8. Records for the Regular Union Army

Unfortunately, service records for the Regular Union Army, Navy, and Marines were never compiled (gathered to- gether) as were those for the Volunteer Union Army. This means that the service records for a member of the Regu- lar Union Army must be gathered from numerous sources, which often requires considerable work. The first thing you need to do is to discover if your Regular Union Army ancestor was an officer. This can be done by looking in

the following volume which lists all officers and gives
some detail on their service.

__F. B. Heitman, HISTORICAL REGISTER AND DICTIONARY AND
REGISTER OF THE US ARMY, 1789-1903, 2 volumes, 57th
Congress, 2nd Session, House Document 446, Serial
Number 4536, Washington, DC, 1903, reprinted by Univer-
sity of IL Press, Urbana, IL, 1965.

If you discover that your ancestor was a commissioned
officer, you may omit the records marked (E) in the
following list, since they apply principally to enlisted
men. If you discover that your ancestor was not a commissioned officer, then you may omit the records marked
(O) in the following list, since they apply principally
to officers. Below are presented some of the main sources of records for Regular Union Army soldiers which are
available in the National Archives. They should be
looked at in the order given.

__(E) National Archives, ENLISTMENT PAPERS FOR THE REGU-
LAR ARMY, Series 2, 1798-1894, Record Group 94, Entry
91, arranged alphabetically by name, take careful note
of the enlistment register entry number and enlistment
date.

__(E) National Archives, MICROFILM COPIES OF REGISTERS OF
ENLISTMENTS FOR THE REGULAR US ARMY, M233, arranged by
initial letter of surname, then chronologically.

__National Archives, MUSTER ROLLS OF THE REGULAR US ARMY,
Record Group 94, Entry 53, arranged by branch of service, then regiment, then by company, then chronologically.

__National Archives, CARDED MEDICAL RECORDS FOR THE
REGULAR US ARMY, arranged by branch of service, then
regiment, then initial letter of surname.

__National Archives, COURT MARTIAL RECORDS FOR THE REGU-
LAR US ARMY, WITH INDEX, indexed by name, then arranged
by case number.

__(E) National Archives, CERTIFICATES OF DISABILITY FOR
THE REGULAR US ARMY, arranged variously.

__(E) National Archives, FINAL STATEMENTS (DEATHS) FOR
THE REGULAR US ARMY, arranged by regiment during groups
of years.

__(O) National Archives, MICROFILM COPIES OF INDEXES TO
LETTERS RECEIVED, ADJUTANT GENERAL'S OFFICE, 1861-89,
M725.

__(O) National Archives, MICROFILM COPIES OF REGISTERS OF
LETTERS RECEIVED, ADJUTANT GENERAL'S OFFICE, M711,

arranged chronologically by years, then by first letter of name.

__(O) National Archives, MICROFILM COPIES OF LETTERS RECEIVED BY THE OFFICE OF THE ADJUTANT GENERAL, 1822-70, M567, and M619, arranged in accordance with the REGISTERS OF LETTERS RECEIVED.

__(O) National Archives, MICROFILM COPIES OF LETTERS SENT BY THE ADJUTANT GENERAL'S OFFICE, WITH INDEX TO EACH VOLUME, 1800-90, M565.

__(O) National Archives, MICROFILM COPIES OF LETTERS RECEIVED BY THE COMMISSION BRANCH OF THE ADJUTANT GENERAL'S OFFICE, 1863-70, M1064.

If you want to take the time, the microfilms M725, M711, M567, M619, and M565 may also be searched for enlisted men since some were included.

9. Records for the Union Navy

Service records for members of the Union Navy, both Regular and Volunteer, must be pieced together by the use of several sources from the National Archives. Your first action should be to look for your veteran in the following book of officers of the regular and Volunteer US Navy.

__E. W. Callahan, LIST OF OFFICERS OF THE NAVY OF THE US AND OF THE MARINE CORPS, 1775-1900, Hamersley and Co., New York, NY, 1901, names listed alphabetically with dates of appointment and service.

If you discover your ancestor was a commissioned officer, you may omit the records marked (E) in the following list, since they apply principally to enlisted men. If you discover that your ancestor was not a commissioned officer, then you may omit the records marked (O) in the following list, since they apply primarily to officers.

__(E) National Archives, MICROFILM COPIES OF INDEXES TO RENDEZVOUS REPORTS (ENLISTMENTS) IN THE US NAVY, 1846-84, T1098 and T1099, these indexes refer to the next two items.

__(E) National Archives, REGISTERS OF ENLISTMENTS IN THE US NAVY, 1845-54, alphabetically by first letter of surname, indexed in T1098 and T1099.

__(E) National Archives, WEEKLY RETURNS OF ENLISTMENTS IN THE US NAVY, 1855-91, listings for 1855-84 indexed in T1098 and T1099.

__(E) National Archives, MUSTER AND PAY ROLLS OF SHORE

ESTABLISHMENTS, 1859-69, arranged alphabetically by
establishment, then chronologically.

__(E) National Archives, MUSTER ROLLS OF VESSELS, 1860-
1900, arranged chronologically in three series, then
alphabetically by name of vessel.

__(E) National Archives, JACKETS (CONTAINING RECORDS) FOR
ENLISTED MEN, 1842-85, arranged alphabetically by name.

__(O) National Archives, COMMISSIONED AND WARRANT OFFIC-
ERS ACCEPTANCES, US REGULAR NAVY, 1804-64, arranged
chronologically and then alphabetically by name.

__(O) National Archives, COMMISSIONED AND WARRANT OFFIC-
ERS ACCEPTANCES, US VOLUNTEER NAVY, 1861-71, arranged
chronologically in series according to rank.

__(O) National Archives, MICROFILMS OF ABSTRACTS OF
SERVICE OF NAVAL OFFICERS, 1798-1893, M330, arranged
chronologically, then alphabetical by name, or indexed.

__(O) National Archives, ABSTRACTS OF SERVICE OF REGULAR
NAVAL OFFICERS, NUMBERED VOLUMES, 1846-1902, indexed in
a loose leaf notebook.

__(O) National Archives, CORRESPONDENCE CONCERNING VOLUN-
TEER NAVAL OFFICERS, 1861-7, and LETTERS SENT TRANSMIT-
TING APPOINTMENTS AND ORDERS, 1861-87, and REGISTERS OF
VOLUNTEER NAVAL OFFICERS HONORABLY DISCHARGED, 1861-70,
some alphabetical by name, some chronologically with
name indexes.

10. Records for the Union Marines

As in the case of the Navy, your first effort is to
consult the following volume to see if your ancestor was
a Marine officer:

__E. W. Callahan, LIST OF OFFICERS OF THE NAVY OF THE US
AND OF THE MARINE CORPS, 1775-1900, Hamersely and Co.,
New York, NY, 1901, names listed alphabetically with
dates of appointment and service.

If you find your forebear to have been a commissioned
officer, you may omit the records marked (E) in the
following list, since they apply principally to enlisted
men. If you discover that your ancestor was not a commissioned officer, then you may omit the records marked
(O) in the following list, since they apply primarily to
officers.

__(E) National Archives, CARD LIST INDEX OF ENLISTED MEN
IN THE US MARINE CORPS, 1798-1941, alphabetically by
name, gives date of enlistment.

__(E) National Archives, SERVICE RECORDS OF US MARINE ENLISTED MEN, 1798-1895, arranged chronologically by year of enlistment, then alphabetically by name, then by month and date of enlistment.

__(E) National Archives, SIZE ROLLS OF US MARINE ENLISTED MEN, 1798-1901, arranged by date of enlistment.

__(E) National Archives, DISCHARGES OF US MARINE ENLISTED MEN, 1829-1927, arranged by date of discharge.

__(O) National Archives, MICROFILM COPIES OF ABSTRACTS OF SERVICE OF NAVAL AND MARINE CORPS OFFICERS, 1798-1893, M330, some of the volumes indexed and others arranged alphabetically.

__(O) National Archives, AGE CERTIFICATES OF NAVY AND MARINE OFFICERS, 1862, 1863, Record Group 24, each year arranged alphabetically.

__National Archives, MARINE CORPS MUSTER ROLLS, 1789-1945, arranged chronologically by month, then by unit.

__National Archives, CERTIFICATE BOOKS OF MARINE OFFICERS AND ENLISTED MEN, 1837-1911, arranged chronologically by date when certificates were made.

11. Records of the Confederate Naval and Marine forces

The chief record holdings in the National Archives relating to Confederate Naval and Marine personnel of the Civil War include service records, hospital and prison records, and muster and pay rolls. As you might suspect, these records are not as complete as the Union records.

__National Archives, MICROFILM COPIES OF SERVICE, HOS-PITAL, AND PRISON RECORDS RELATING TO CONFEDERATE NAVAL AND MARINE PERSONNEL, M260, arranged alphabetically in a Naval series, and alphabetically in a Marine series.

__National Archives, MUSTER ROLLS AND PAYROLLS OF SHIPS AND SHORE ESTABLISHMENTS OF THE CONFEDERATE NAVY, arranged by ship and establishment.

__National Archives, MICROFILM COPIES OF SUBJECT FILE OF THE CONFEDERATE STATES NAVY, 1861-5, M1091, arranged according to subject, then chronologically.

12. Burial and headstone records

There are a number of Civil War veteran burial records in the National Archives, most of them relating to Union men. The key to these records is in a card index which lists practically all soldiers who were buried in national cemeteries and federally-supervised cemeteries from 1861 to the present. This card index is located as follows:

__The Cemetery Service, National Cemetery System, Veterans Administration, 810 Vermont Ave., NW, Washington, DC 20422.

You may request a search of the index by mail, but be sure and accompany your request with an SASE. With the location information obtained from the card index, you can then look into the following records:

__National Archives, UNION SOLDIERS BURIED AT NATIONAL CEMETERIES, mainly 1861-5, arranged by state of burial, then there are three lists under each state (one by cemetery, a second by military unit, a third by first letter of surname).

__National Archives, MICROFILM COPIES OF REGISTER OF CONFEDERATE SOLDIERS, SAILORS, AND CITIZENS WHO DIED IN FEDERAL PRISONS AND MILITARY HOSPITALS IN THE NORTH, M918, alphabetical by name of prison or hospital, then alphabetical by name.

Also consult a 27-volumed series of books:

__ROLL OF HONOR, US Quartermaster Dept., Washington, DC, 1865-71, burial lists of Union soldiers, arranged by state, then cemetery, then alphabetically by name of soldier.

Civil War servicemen who were buried in private cemeteries could have government-donated headstones if their heirs applied for them. The applications have been kept and a card index to them is available:

__National Archives, CARD INDEX TO APPLICATIONS FOR HEADSTONES, 1879-1903, arranged alphabetically by name.

__National Archives, APPLICATIONS FOR HEADSTONES, 1879-1964, several series, each arranged by state of burial, then county, then cemetery.

13. Civil War civilian records

Numerous records in the National Archives refer to civilians during the Civil War and during the years shortly after. Most of them refer to civilians in the South, but there is a long set of internal revenue tax assessments for persons in the north during 1862-6:

__National Archives, MICROFILM COPIES OF INTERNAL REVENUE ASSESSMENT LISTS, 1862-6, M754 through M795, by states, then assessment district (county).

Among the more important Confederate civilian records are those kept by the Union Provost Marshals. The marshals

were military police who kept law and order in the southern areas which were conquered by the Union forces. They
kept records on spies, disloyal citizens, prisoners, persons granted passage, people taking oaths of allegiance,
individuals granted paroles and pardons, those violating
military orders, and personnel accused of civil crimes.
The records are:

__National Archives, MICROFILM COPIES OF UNION PROVOST
MARSHALS' FILE OF PAPERS RELATING TO INDIVIDUAL
CIVILIANS, M345, alphabetical by name of civilian or
soldier.

__National Archives, MICROFILM COPIES OF UNION PROVOST
MARSHALS' FILE OF PAPERS RELATING TO TWO OR MORE CIV-
ILIANS, M416, records can be located from cross references in the previously-named documents relating to
individuals.

Many Confederate civilians are also mentioned in the
correspondence of the War Department of the Confederacy.
The first two items mentioned below are indexes which
lead to the actual correspondence in the third, fourth,
and fifth items:

__National Archives, MICROFILM COPY OF INDEX TO LETTERS
RECEIVED BY THE CONFEDERATE SECRETARY OF WAR, 1861-5,
M409, alphabetical by name.

__National Archives, MICROFILM COPY OF INDEX TO LETTERS
RECEIVED BY THE CONFEDERATE ADJUTANT AND INSPECTOR
GENERAL AND THE CONFEDERATE QUARTERMASTER GENERAL,
1861-5, M410, alphabetical by name.

__National Archives, MICROFILM COPY OF LETTERS RECEIVED
BY THE CONFEDERATE SECRETARY OF WAR, 1861-5, M437.

__National Archives, MICROFILM COPY OF LETTERS RECEIVED
BY THE CONFEDERATE ADJUTANT AND INSPECTOR GENERAL,
1861-5, M474.

__National Archives, MICROFILM COPY OF LETTERS RECEIVED
BY THE CONFEDERATE QUARTERMASTER GENERAL, 1861-5, M469.

__National Archives, CONFEDERATE PAPERS RELATING TO
CITIZENS OR BUSINESS FIRMS, M346, includes card abstracts on citizens and civilian employees.

Between 1863 and 1868 pardon or amnesty was granted
by the US to participants in the rebellion if they would
take an oath of allegiance. After 1868, practically all
remaining participants were pardoned without the oath
requirement. Among the most important of these records
are:

National Archives, AMNESTY OATHS RELATING TO INDIVI-
DUALS, 1863-6, Record Group 59, arranged by state, then
alphabetically by first two letters of surname.
National Archives, AMNESTY OATHS RELATING TO TWO OR
MORE PERSONS, 1863-6, Record Group 59, arranged by
state, then numerically, access by cross references in
the above document.
National Archives, OATHS OF ALLEGIANCE TO THE FEDERAL
GOVERNMENT, Record Group 59, arranged by state, then
alphabetically. Persons granted amnesty by President
Johnson before 1868.

Between 1865-7, large numbers were granted amnesty,
but high-ranking civilians and military men, and those
with more than $20,000 of property had to apply to the
President. These applications along with an index are:
National Archives, MICROFILM COPY OF CASE FILES OF
APPLICATIONS FROM FORMER CONFEDERATES FOR PRESIDENTIAL
PARDONS, 1865-7, WITH INDEX, 1865-7, M1003, arranged by
state, then alphabetically by name.
The following records are available on pardons:
National Archives, PERSONS ACCEPTING AMNESTY PARDONS,
1865-7, and PRESIDENTIAL PARDONS FOR CONFEDERATES,
1865-6, both in record Group 59, with a consolidated
name index.
Lists of most of those pardoned were also published in
several of the volumes in the US Congressional Document
Series. The volume series numbers are 1263, 1289, 1293,
1311, 1314, and 1330.

During 1871-80, the US Southern Claims Commission
examined claims for property and services rendered the US
Army by southern citizens who remained loyal to the US.
These are indexed in the publication:
US House of Representatives, THE CONSOLIDATED INDEX OF
CLAIMS REPORTED BY THE COMMISSIONERS OF CLAIMS TO THE
HOUSE OF REPRESENTATIVES FROM 1871-80, Government
Printing Office, Washington, DC, 1982.
This index leads to:
National Archives, APPROVED CLAIMS REPORTED BY THE
COMMISSIONERS OF CLAIMS, 1871-80, Record Group 217,
arranged by state, then by county, then alphabetically
by name.
National Archives, DISALLOWED CLAIMS REPORTED BY THE
COMMISSIONERS OF CLAIMS, 1871-80, Record Group 233.

Loyal citizens in Union states who supplied materials and services for the US forces also filed claims for payment after the War.

__National Archives, QUARTERMASTER CLAIMS ARISING FROM THE CIVIL WAR, 1861-70, Record Group 92, 68 register volumes, each with name index, references lead to claims files containing documents.

There are also abundant records of civilian employees of the US War Department and the Confederate Government during the War years. For details see the book:

__National Archives Staff, GUIDE TO GENEALOGICAL RESEARCH IN THE NATIONAL ARCHIVES, The National Archives and Records Service, Washington, DC, 1982, sections 14.2.6 and 14.4.

Chapter 3

NATIONAL PUBLICATIONS

1. Libraries

In addition to the numerous records in archives, a large number of books containing information on individuals in the Civil War has been published. These are generally available in larger libraries or can be borrowed through smaller libraries on interlibrary loan. The interlibrary loan is an absolute boon to genealogical researchers who do not have ready access to a large library. When you discover that a volume you require is not in your library, all you need to do is to ask the librarian to borrow it for you from some other library on interlibrary loan. Or if you know which pages in an unavailable volume you need, you can request photocopies of these pages on the interlibrary loan system. There is a small charge for these services, ordinarily no more than a few dollars.

2. Field reports

Just before the Civil War ended, the US government began to collect all army field reports, battle correspondence, tactical plans, communications, military orders, and memorandums which had been written as the military operations of the War were carried out. These have been published as 128 volumes of records containing almost 140,000 pages. They may be found in many city, college, and university libraries. The reports, in the large, are copies of first-hand observations made by officers of the army and reported to superiors. Many persons are mentioned in the reports, but the higher a soldier's rank, the more likely it will be that you will find him. This is because officers generally did the reporting. But even so, many enlisted men are mentioned, especially if they were cited for valiant action, wounded, or killed. The last of the 128 volumes is a complete alphabetized index. This is especially valuable if you know nothing about the state or military unit of your ancestor, since references in this index are not gathered by states. You may very well be able to associate your veteran with a specific state and a specific army military unit through the references in these volumes. The Index is:

__INDEX, OFFICIAL RECORDS OF THE UNION AND CONFEDERATE ARMIES IN THE WAR OF THE REBELLION, Government Printing Office, Washington, DC, 1901.

References in the OFFICIAL RECORDS INDEX involve three symbols, a Roman numeral (I, II, III, or IV), an Arabic numeral (such as 7 or 21 or 42), and sometimes a plus sign (+). The 128 volumes are divided into 4 series and the Roman numerals refer to these. The Arabic numerals refer to the volumes in the series, and the plus sign (+) indicates that there is a correction shown in the back of the INDEX. When you have located a reference (such as II, 5), take the proper series (II) and the proper volume (5) and look into the separate index in the back of that volume for the name being sought. There you will find the page reference, which will permit you to locate the document. Be very careful, since many volumes are split into two or three parts, and the indexes of all of them must be examined. The volumes are:

__OFFICIAL RECORDS OF THE UNION AND CONFEDERATE ARMIES IN THE WAR OF THE REBELLION, Government Printing Office, Washington, DC, 1901, 128 volumes with the Index volume.

A set of 31 volumes very similar to the above army volumes has been published for the navies. The same general remarks apply to this set, including the nature of the Index, which is the last volume.

__OFFICIAL RECORDS OF THE UNION AND CONFEDERATE NAVIES IN THE WAR OF THE REBELLION, Government Printing Office, Washington, DC, 1922, 31 volumes with the Index volume.

There is a very detailed atlas which accompanies these two sets of volumes. Contained in it are excellent detailed maps of the military operations of the War. It is:

__C. D. Cowles, THE OFFICIAL ATLAS OF THE CIVIL WAR, Yoseloff, New York, NY, 1891-5 (reprint 1958).

Finally, your attention should be called to some very valuable supplementary publications. These are guides and indexes to all the materials in OFFICIAL RECORDS - ARMIES and the OFFICIAL ATLAS which have to do with particular battles, encounters, excursions, missions, or campaigns. No personal names are listed, but by looking up the name of a battle in which your ancestor fought, you will find references to all documents and maps which deal with it:

MILITARY OPERATIONS OF THE CIVIL WAR, A GUIDE-INDEX TO THE OFFICIAL RECORDS OF THE UNION AND CONFEDERATE ARMIES, National Archives and Record Service, Washington, DC, 1968 ff.

3. Pension and Census Lists

There appeared in 1883 a 5-volumed set of books listing holders of US military pensions as of the first of the year 1883. There are over 300,000 entries, each one giving the veteran's name and address, the reason for the pension, and the date on which the pension began. Only pensioners by virtue of death or disability in service are listed. The volumes list entries by state and then by county, so you need to know where your veteran was living in 1883. The books are:

LIST OF PENSIONERS ON THE ROLLS, JANUARY 1, 1883, Senate Executive Document 84, 47th Congress, 2nd session, Genealogical Publishing Co., Baltimore, MD, 1883 (reprint 1970), 5 volumes, Serials 2078-82.

Even though the general Census of 1890 did not survive a fire in 1921, some of the census returns listing Union Civil War veterans and widows of deceased veterans survived. The records for the states of KY through WY are available, but those for KY are incomplete. The records are arranged by state and then by county, so you need to know the county in which your veteran or his widow was living in 1890. The records include name of veteran, name of widow if applicable, rank, company, regiment or ship, enlistment date, discharge date, length of service, address, and the nature of any disability. These Census schedules are available on microfilm from the National Archives. Have your librarian borrow the microfilm for your state and county so that you can search it for your veteran:

National Archives, SPECIAL SCHEDULES OF THE 11TH CENSUS (1890) ENUMERATING UNION VETERANS AND WIDOWS OF UNION VETERANS OF THE CIVIL WAR, M123, 118 rolls, Washington, DC.

State indexes for these schedules are being published. They are now available for many states and others are in preparation. They are provided in both printed and microfiche formats:

__1890 KY (LA, ME, MD, MA, MI, MN, MS, NY, SC, TX) CENSUS INDEXES OF CIVIL WAR VETERANS OR THEIR WIDOWS, Index Publishing, Salt Lake City, UT, 1984-.

__1890 DC (KY, LA, MS, MT, NE, NH, NM, NC, ND, OK, OR, RI, SC, UT, VT, VA, WA, WV, WY) CENSUS INDEXES OF CIVIL WAR VETERANS, Accelerated Indexing Systems, North Salt Lake, UT, 1980-.

4. Burial indexes

You will find in many libraries a couple of works listing Union burial places. The most important of these is:

__ROLL OF HONOR, US Quartermaster's Department, Washington, DC, 1866-71.

Here are to be found thousands of entries of Union soldiers who were buried in public and private cemeteries during the Civil War. The entries are under states, then under the names of the cemeteries, and then alphabetically. The date of death is shown along with the burial site. Another work which may be consulted but is generally of less use is:

__S. L. Pompey, BURIAL LISTS OF MEMBERS OF UNION AND CONFEDERATE MILITARY UNITS, Kingsburg, CA, 1971.

5. Officer rosters, lists, biographies

As you have no doubt realized, Union and Confederate army and naval officers generated more records than their colleagues in the non-commissioned ranks. In keeping with this, there are quite a number of printed collections of data (rosters, lists, biographies) on these officers. Some of the more useful ones will be described here so that you can look into them if your ancestor was an officer or if you are interested in the officers of your ancestor's military unit.

In order to understand and make proper use of the rosters, lists, and biographies relating to Union officers, you need to understand the difference between regular officers and volunteer officers. Regular officers are professionals who have made the military their career. Volunteer officers are civilians who joined the

armed forces in the time of military crisis. Biographies
of regular army officers may be found in:

__OFFICIAL ARMY REGISTER 1861-5, US Adjutant General's
Office, Washington, DC, 7 volumes, 1861-5.

Another volume in which you will find biographies of
regular army officers is:

__F. B. Heitman, HISTORICAL REGISTER AND DICTIONARY OF
THE US ARMY FROM ITS BEGINNING SEPTEMBER 19, 1789 TO
MARCH 2, 1903, Univ. of IL Press, Urbana, IL, 1903
(reprint 1965).

Another volume dealing with regular army officers, but
not quite so complete is:

__T. H. S. Hamersly, editor, COMPLETE REGULAR ARMY
REGISTER OF THE US FOR 100 YEARS (1779-1879), Hamersly,
Washington, DC, 1881.

A final book which lists both army and navy regular
officers is:

__W. H. Powell, OFFICERS OF THE ARMY AND NAVY (REGULAR)
WHO SERVED IN THE CIVIL WAR, Hamersly Co., Philadelphia, PA, 1892.

Both regular and volunteer officers are listed in:

__L. R. Hamersly and Co., publishers, OFFICERS OF THE
ARMY AND NAVY (REGULAR AND VOLUNTEER) WHO SERVED IN THE
CIVIL WAR, Hamersly Co., Philadelphia, PA, 1894.

An outstanding collection of biographical sketches
of volunteer Union officers is contained in the following
8-volumed set:

__OFFICIAL ARMY REGISTER OF THE VOLUNTEER FORCE OF THE US
ARMY FOR THE YEARS 1861-2-3-4-5, US Adjutant General's
Office, Washington, DC, 8 volumes, 1865-7.

A book with similar sorts of listings which is also
recommended for your perusal in seeking information on
volunteer Union officers is:

__W. H. Powell. OFFICERS OF THE ARMY AND NAVY (VOLUNTEER)
WHO SERVED IN THE CIVIL WAR, Hamersly Co., Philadelphia, PA, 1893.

In addition to the two books by Powell and the one
by L. Hamersly listed above, there are several works by
T. H. S. Hamersly and one by L. Hamersly which deal with
Union Naval officers:

__L. Hamersly, THE RECORD OF LIVING OFFICERS OF THE US
NAVY AND MARINE CORPS, Hamersly Co., Philadelphia, PA,
1870.

__T. H. S. Hamersly, COMPLETE GENERAL NAVY REGISTER OF THE USA FROM 1776 TO 1887, Washington, DC, 1880-1.

__T. H. S. Hamersly, GENERAL REGISTER OF THE US NAVY AND MARINE CORPS, 1782-1882, INCLUDING VOLUNTEER OFFICERS, Washington, DC, 1882.

There are other editions and other forms of the latter two books which carry essentially the same information. For information on Confederate Naval and Marine officers, consult:

__OFFICERS IN THE CONFEDERATE STATES NAVY, 1861-5, US Naval Records Office, Washington, DC, 1898.

__C. A. Evans, CONFEDERATE MILITARY HISTORY: Naval and Marine Officers, January 1, 1864, Volume 12, pp. 110-9.

__R. W. Donnelly, BIOGRAPHICAL SKETCHES OF COMMISSIONED OFFICERS OF THE CONFEDERATE STATES MARINE CORPS, The Author, Alexandria, VA, 1973.

__REGISTER OF OFFICERS OF THE CONFEDERATE STATES NAVY, Carroll Co., Mattituck, NJ, 1983.

Four books which list Confederate Army officers of the Civil War are:

__GENERAL OFFICERS OF THE CONFEDERATE ARMY, Carroll Co., Mattituck, NJ, 1983.

__LIST OF FIELD OFFICERS, REGIMENTS, AND BATTALIONS IN THE CONFEDERATE ARMY, Carroll Co., Mattituck, NJ, 1983.

__LIST OF STAFF OFFICERS OF THE CONFEDERATE ARMY, Carroll Co., Mattituck, NJ, 1983.

__B. E. Wilson, GENERAL OFFICERS OF THE CONFEDERACY, The Author, Baytown, TX, 1976.

6. Confederate veterans' publications

In 1869, a group of Confederate veterans organized the Southern Historical Society with the aim of collecting, classifying, and publishing Confederate military records and recollections. Fifty-two volumes of all sorts of materials were published including battle descriptions, troop maneuvers, camp incidents, casualty lists, unit and ship rosters, promotions, correspondence, diary entries, personal memoirs, sick lists, hospital and prison records, Confederate Congressional records, minutes of numerous post-war meetings, and many other documents. These 52 books provide a very useful and informative source of Confederate information, second in value only to the OFFICIAL RECORDS:

SOUTHERN HISTORICAL SOCIETY PAPERS, Volumes 1-52, Southern Historical Society, Richmond, VA, 1876-1959.

This exceptionally valuable set of volumes has been comprehensively indexed. You should consult this index for your Confederate ancestor's name, and for materials relating to his military unit or ship, the battles in which he participated, and the places where he was stationed or which he passed through or passed by (rivers, creeks, counties, towns, hamlets, prisons). The military units from a given state are listed under the name of the state followed by the word Troops. For example, if you are looking for the 8th Reserve Infantry Regiment of Georgia, you should look under Georgia Troops (C.S.) for Infantry Regiments. Under this you will find the 8th Reserve. References to US military units would appear under Georgia Troops (U.S.).

J. I. Robertson, Jr., editor, SOUTHERN HISTORICAL SOCIETY PAPERS INDEX, 2 volumes, Kraus, Millwood, NY, 1980.

Once materials (names, units, ships, places) have been located in the index, they can then be looked up in the appropriate volumes.

Even if your Civil War ancestor was not a Confederate, you should not fail to use this set of reference works. It is, of course, extremely unlikely that Union names would appear, but the battles, prisons, and places with which your Union serviceman was associated should be sought out in the index. Valuable details which are pertinent to your Northern veteran's military career can often be found.

Another series of publications which needs to be mentioned is a magazine which gives a great deal of biographical data on Confederates, both army and navy, both officers and non-commissioned soldiers and sailors:

THE CONFEDERATE VETERAN, Nashville, TN, over 40 volumes published 1893-1932.

Fortunately, there is a published overall index to the 40 volumes. There are over 165,000 different names listed.

L. H. Manarin, THE CONFEDERATE VETERAN INDEX, Broadfoot Publishing Co., Wilmington, NC, 1987, 3 volumes.

A further series of valuable volumes consists of original reports by Confederate physicians and therefore

contains numerous case histories of Confederate service men. In many of these histories, there are biographical data. In addition, sizable listings of Confederate medical personnel are given. These volumes are:
__CONFEDERATE STATES MEDICAL AND SURGICAL JOURNAL, 14 issues, January 1864 through February 1865, reprint by Scarecrow Press, Metuchen, NJ, 1976.
There is a somewhat similar publication covering both Confederate and Union medical cases. This set of volumes contains many lists of soldiers receiving medical treatment:
__US War Department, MEDICAL AND SURGICAL HISTORY OF THE WAR OF THE REBELLION, Government Printing Office, Washington, DC, 1883.

7. Civil War claims

During the Civil War there were many residents of the Confederate States (AL, AR, FL, GA, LA, MS, NC, SC, TN, TX, VA) and of WV who remained loyal to the US and opposed the claims of the Confederacy. Some fled to the North, but most stayed and did their best to get along with their neighbors, usually by keeping a low profile. When the Union invaded the South, the Federal troops sometimes obtained food and supplies from these pro-Union Southerners. In some instances payment was given, but ordinarily only a receipt was given and it was promised that payment would be made after the end of the War.

On 03 March 1871 laws were passed which set up the Southern Claims Commission to receive claims of loyalists who lived in the Confederate States. Over 22,000 claims were filed by pro-Union Southerners. Only about 7000 of the claims were judged to be legitimate, but all the documents relating to all 22,000 of them are in the National Archives. All sorts of genealogically valuable papers are in the files. Some of the kinds of documents which may be found are: wills, birth records, lists of family members, family letters, court cases, testimonies of witnesses (both Union and Confederate), and affidavits filed by neighbors, local leaders, political office holders and professional persons (such as ministers, lawyers, and doctors). In fact, if you will take the time, you may uncover material concerning your family in claims filed by other persons in the same county.

These claims have been indexed in the following volumes:
__ G. B. Mills, CIVIL WAR CLAIMS IN THE SOUTH, Aegean Park Press, Laguna Hills, CA, 1980-1, 2 volumes.
If you locate your ancestor in the index, or if you want to look at documents filed by other persons in the same county, send the complete index listing (state, county, case number), the designation RG56 (standing for record Group 56), and inquire as to the cost of copying the original documents to:
__ Legislative, Judicial, and Fiscal Branch, National Archives, Pennsylvania Ave. between 7th and 9th Sts., Washington, DC 20408.

8. Prison lists

A number of books have been printed which list prisoners in various prisons of the Union and of the Confederacy. Among the major books presenting data on Union prisoners in Confederate prisons are:
__ A. O. Abbott, PRISON LIFE IN THE SOUTH, Harper and Brothers, New York, NY, 1866. Officers in prison in Columbia, SC 1864-5.
__ D. Atwater, UNION SOLDIERS BURIED AT ANDERSONVILLE, NY Tribune Association, New York, NY, 1868. 12000 names.
__ C. D. Berry, THE LOSS OF THE SULTANA, Thorp, Lansing, MI, 1892. Steamer sinking, over 1500 exchanged Union prisoners lost.
__ A. Cooper, IN AND OUT OF REBEL PRISONS, Oliphant, Oswego, NY, 1888. 35 pages of officers imprisoned in Macon, GA 1864.
__ W. W. Glazier, THE CAPTURE, THE PRISON PEN, AND THE ESCAPE, Goodwin, Hartford, CT, 1867. Officers in Libby Prison (Richmond) and at Columbia, SC 1864.
__ W. C. Harris, PRISON LIFE IN THE TOBACCO WAREHOUSE AT RICHMOND, Childs, Philadelphia, PA, 1862. Soldiers in prison at Richmond, VA 1861-2.
__ J. Hawes, CAHABA, A STORY OF CAPTIVE BOYS IN BLUE, Burr Printing House, New York, NY, 1888. Soldiers in prison at Cahaba, AL 1863-5.
__ A. B. Isham and others, PRISONERS OF WAR AND MILITARY PRISONS, Lyman and Cushing, Cincinnati, OH, 1890. Over 2000 officers in various prisons 1864-5.
__ W. H. Jeffrey, RICHMOND PRISONS, 1861-2, Republican Press, St. Johnsbury, VT, 1893. About 4000 names.

C. Lamman, JOURNAL OF ALFRED ELY, PRISONER OF WAR IN RICHMOND, Appleton and Co., New York, NY, 1862. Soldiers in Confederate prisons as of 25 November 1861. 75 pages of listings.

PA AT ANDERSONVILLE AND SALISBURY, Aughinbaugh, Harrisburg, PA, 1909-12, 2 volumes. Prison survivors.

J. L. Ransom, ANDERSONVILLE DIARY, Haskell House, New York, 1881 (1974). Camp Asylum Prison, Columbia, SC.

G. E. Sabre, NINETEEN MONTHS A PRISONER OF WAR, American News Co., New York, NY, 1865.

S. Schwartz, TWENTY-TWO MONTHS A PRISONER OF WAR, Nelson Publishing Co., St. Louis, MO, 1892. Soldiers in prison in TX 1861-3.

US Christian Commission, FEDERAL DEAD BURIED FROM LIBBY, BELLE ISLE, DANVILLE, AND CAMP LAWTON PRISONS, AT CITY POINT, AND BEFORE PETERSBURG AND RICHMOND, The Commission, Philadelphia, PA, 1865. Thousands of prisoners listed.

Among the larger published compilations of Confederate prisoners in Union prison camps are:

J. Barbiere, SCRAPS FROM THE PRISON TABLE AT CAMP CHASE AND JOHNSON'S ISLAND, Davis, Doylestown, PA, 1868. 57 pages of Confederate prisoners.

E. W. Beitzel, POINT LOOKOUT PRISON CAMP, The Author, Abell, MD, 1972. Over 3000 prisoners who died in camp.

CONFEDERATES WHO DIED AT CAMP DOUGLAS, CHICAGO, IL, 1862-5, Gray, Kalamazoo, MI, 1968. Over 4400.

B. England, CONFEDERATE SOLDIERS WHO ARE BURIED AT ROCK ISLAND ARSENAL, The Arsenal, Rock Island, IL, 1985.

F. Fuzzlebug, PRISON LIFE DURING THE REBELLION, Funk's Sons, Singers Glen, VA, 1869. 600 Confederate officers in prison at Morris Island 1864.

C. W. Holmes, THE ELMIRA PRISON CAMP, 1864-5, Putnam's Sons, New York, NY, 1912. Almost 3000 Confederate prisoner burials.

Frances T. Ingmire, CONFEDERATES WHO DIED IN FEDERAL PRISONS AND HOSPITALS, Ingmire Publications, St. Louis, MO, 1985. Very large list.

W. H. Knauss, THE STORY OF CAMP CHASE, ITS CEMETERY, AND OTHER CEMETERIES, Methodist Episcopal Church, Nashville, TN, 1906. Confederate burials at Camp Chase, Antietam, South Mountain, and Monocacy.

J. C. Poe, THE RAVING FOE, Longhorn Press, Eastland, TX, 1967. Over 1200 prisoners on Johnson's Island, Lake Erie.

Chapter 4

STATE PUBLICATIONS

1. Introduction

In addition to many publications (both books and microfilms) which the federal government has made available, most of the states involved in the Civil War have issued publications which are of use to genealogists. It is usually true that if you have written to a State Archives requesting information, they will have probably used state publications in their search for your ancestor. The most likely items for them to have looked into are state rosters and for the Confederate states pension records. However, unless you have specifically requested it, they probably will not have examined state military histories. These three types of state publications (rosters, regimental histories, and Confederate pension records) will be treated in this chapter.

2. State rosters

A roster is a list giving each person's name and his affiliation. Many states have published or commissioned the publication of volumes which list the names of personnel from the state who served in the Civil War. Sometimes only officers are listed, but often all known personnel will be included. Among the better ones are:

AL: S. L. Pompey, MUSTER LIST OF THE AL CONFEDERATE TROOPS, The Author, Independence, CA, 1965.

AR: A. W. Bishop, REPORT OF THE ADJUTANT GENERAL OF THE STATE OF AR FOR THE PERIOD OF THE LATE REBELLION AND TO NOVEMBER 1, 1866, Government Printing Office, Washington, DC, 1867 (Union militia and volunteers); AR CSA SOLDIERS, 1911 CENSUS OF CONFEDERATE VETERANS, AR Ancestors, Hot Springs, AR, 1981-2, 3 volumes.

CA: R. H. Orton, RECORDS OF CA MEN IN THE WAR OF THE REBELLION, 1861-7, CA State Printer, Sacramento, CA, 1890; to be used with J. C. Parker, A PERSONAL NAME INDEX TO RECORDS OF CA MEN IN THE WAR OF THE REBELLION, 1861-7, Gale Research Co., Detroit, MI, 1978.

CO: CO Adjutant General's Office, BIENNIAL REPORTS OF THE ADJUTANT GENERAL, 1861-5, Adjutant General's Office, Denver, CO, 1866.

44

_CT: CT Adjutant General's Office, RECORD OF SERVICE OF CT MEN IN THE ARMY AND NAVY OF THE US DURING THE WAR OF THE REBELLION, 1861-5, Case, Lockwood, and Brainerd, Hartford, CT, 1889 (no index).

_DE: J. T. Scharf, HISTORY OF DE, 1609-1888, Richards & Co., Philadelphia, PA, 1888 (Appendix to volume 1 contains muster rolls).

_FL: F. L. Robertson, SOLDIERS OF FL IN THE SEMINOLE INDIAN, CIVIL, AND SPANISH-AMERICAN WARS, Democrat Book and Job Print, Live Oak, FL, 1909 (Muster rolls on pages 33-338 of part 2).

_GA: L. Henderson, ROSTER OF CONFEDERATE SOLDIERS OF GA, 1861-5, Longino and Porter, Hapeville, GA, 1959-64, 6 volumes (Rosters of infantry only), indexed by J. S. Brightwell, INDEX TO THE ROSTER OF THE CONFEDERATE SOLDIERS OF GA, 1861-5, Reprint Co., Spartanburg, SC, 1982; A. D. Candler, THE CONFEDERATE RECORDS OF THE STATE OF GA, GA Legislature, Atlanta, GA, 5 volumes, 1909-11.

_IL: J. N. Reece, REPORT OF THE ADJUTANT GENERAL OF THE STATE OF IL, Phillips, Springfield, IL, 1900-2 (Volumes 1-8 deal with Civil War).

_IN: W. H. H. Terrell, IN ADJUTANT GENERAL'S REPORT, Conner, Indianapolis, IN, 1865-9 (Volumes 2-8 contain rosters; index in IN State Archives).

_IA: W. H. Thrift, ROSTER AND RECORD OF IA SOLDIERS IN THE WAR OF THE REBELLION, 1861-6, English, Des Moines, IA, 1908-11 (First 5 volumes pertain to Civil War), and L. D. Ingersoll, IA AND THE REBELLION, Lippincott, Philadelphia, PA, 1867.

_KS: P. S. Noble, REPORT OF ADJUTANT GENERAL'S OFFICE OF STATE OF KS, 1861-5, KS State Print Co., Topeka, KS, 1867-70, 1 volumes.

_KY: A. Harris, REPORT OF ADJUTANT GENERAL OF KY, CON-FEDERATE KY VOLUNTEERS, 1861-5, State Journal Co., Frankfort, KY, 1915-8, 2 volumes.

_LA: A. B. Booth, RECORDS OF LA CONFEDERATE SOLDIERS AND LA CONFEDERATE COMMANDS, Military Record Commission, New Orleans, LA, 1920, 3 volumes.

_ME: ADJUTANT GENERAL'S ANNUAL REPORTS, 1861-6, Stevens and Sayward, Augusta, ME, 1862-7, 7 volumes, and ALPHABETICAL INDEX OF ME VOLUNTEERS OF THE WAR OF 1861, Augusta, ME, 1867.

_MD: W. W. Goldsborough, THE MD LINE IN THE CONFEDERATE ARMY, 1861-5, Kennikat Press, Port Washington, NY (1900), 1972; L. A. Wilmer, HISTORY AND ROSTER OF MD

VOLUNTEERS, WAR OF 1861-5, Guggenheimer, Weil, and Co., Baltimore, MD, 1898-9, 2 volumes; D. D. Hartzler, MARYLANDERS IN THE CONFEDERACY, Family Line Publications, Silver Spring, MD, 1986. (About 12000 names.).

MA: Adjutant General's Office, MA SOLDIERS, SAILORS, AND MARINES IN THE CIVIL WAR, Norwood Press, Norwood, MA, 1931, 8 volumes plus index to Army records which was published in 1937 (Navy and Marine records not indexed).

MI: G. H. Brown, RECORD OF SERVICE OF MI VOLUNTEERS IN THE CIVIL WAR, 1861-5, 46 volumes, Ihling and Everard, Kalamazoo, MI, 1905; C. C. Vaughn, ALPHABETICAL GENERAL INDEX, Wynkoop Hallenbeck Crawford, Lansing, MI, 1915.

MN: Board of Commissioners, MN IN THE CIVIL AND INDIAN WARS, 1861-5, Pioneer Press, St. Paul, MN, 1890-3, 2 volumes, and INDEX TO THE ROSTERS, MN Historical Society, St. Paul, MN, 1936.

MS: J. C. Rietti, MILITARY ANNALS OF MS, Reprint Co., Spartanburg, SC, 1976.

MO: S. L. Pompey, MUSTER LISTS OF THE MO CONFEDERATES, Historical and Genealogical Publishing Co., Independence, CA, 1965.

NE: E. S. Dudley, ROSTER OF NE VOLUNTEERS FROM 1861 TO 1869, Adjutant General, Hastings, NE, 1888, and HISTORY OF THE STATE OF NE, Western Historical Co., Chicago, IL, 1882.

NV: J. Cradlebaugh, ANNUAL REPORT OF THE ADJUTANT GENERAL FOR 1865, Carson City, NV, 1866, and C. E. Laughton, ROSTER OF VOLUNTEERS, Biennial Report of NV, Carson City, 1884, pp. 29-55.

NH: A. D. Ayling, REVISED REGISTER OF THE SOLDIERS AND SAILORS OF NH IN THE WAR OF THE REBELLION, 1861-5, Evans, Concord, NH, 1895.

NJ: W. S. Stryker, RECORDS OF OFFICERS AND MEN OF NJ IN THE CIVIL WAR, 1861-5, Murphy, Trenton, NJ, 1876.

NM: M. H. Hall, THE CONFEDERATE ARMY OF NM, Presidial Press, Austin, TX, 1978.

NY: F. Phisterer, NY IN THE WAR OF THE REBELLION, 1861-5, Lyon, Albany, NY, 5 volumes and index volume, and Adjutant General, A RECORD OF COMMISSIONED OFFICERS, NON-COMMISSIONED OFFICERS, AND PRIVATES OF THE REGIMENTS WHICH WERE ORGANIZED IN THE STATE OF NY, Albany, NY, 1864-8, 8 volumes, and Adjutant General, REGISTERS OF NY REGIMENTS IN THE WAR OF THE REBELLION, 1894-1906, 46 volumes.

__NC: W. T. Jordan and L. H. Manarin, NC TROOPS, 1861-5, NC State Archives, Raleigh, NC, 1966-83, 17 volumes, and J. W. Moore, ROSTER OF NC TROOPS IN THE WAR BETWEEN THE STATES, Ashe and Gatling, Raleigh, NC, 1882 (Card index in NC Archives).

__ND & SD (Dakota Territory): US Congress, DAKOTA MILITIA IN THE WAR OF 1862, 58th Congress, 2nd Session, Senate Document No. 241, Washington, DC, 1904.

__OH: OH Roster Commission, OFFICIAL ROSTER OF THE SOL-DIERS OF THE STATE OF OH IN THE WAR OF THE REBELLION, 1861-6, Werner, Akron, OH, 1886-95, 12 volumes, (WPA index made in 1938, Navy personnel in volume 12).

__OR: C. A. Reed, REPORT OF THE ADJUTANT GENERAL OF THE STATE OF OR FOR THE YEARS 1865-6, Salem, OR, 1866.

__PA: S. P. Bates, HISTORY OF PA VOLUNTEERS, 1861-5, Singerly, Harrisburg, PA, 1969-71, 5 volumes.

__RI: E. Dyer, ADJUTANT GENERAL'S ANNUAL REPORT FOR THE YEAR 1865, Providence, RI, 1893-5 (revised edition).

__SC: A. S. Salley, SC TROOPS IN CONFEDERATE SERVICE, State Archives, Columbia, SC, 1913-60, 3 volumes (partial listing only).

__TN: Civil War Centennial Commission, TENNESSEANS IN THE CIVIL WAR, Nashville, TN, 1964, volume 2.

__VT: T. S. Peck, REVISED ROSTER OF VT VOLUNTEERS AND LISTS OF VERMONTERS WHO SERVED IN THE ARMY AND NAVY OF THE US DURING THE WAR OF THE REBELLION, 1861-6, Watchman Publ. Co., Montpelier, VT, 1892.

__WV: WV ADJUTANT GENERAL'S ANNUAL REPORTS OF THE YEARS ENDING DECEMBER 31, 1864-5, Wheeling, WV, 1865-6, and T. F. Lang, LOYAL WV FROM 1861 to 1865, Deutsch Publ. Co., Baltimore, MD, 1895.

__WI: Adjutant General, ROSTERS OF WI VOLUNTEERS, WAR OF THE REBELLION, 1861-5, Democrat Print Co., Madison, WI, 1914, 2 volumes, and WI VOLUNTEERS OF THE REBELLION, 1861-5, arranged alphabetically, Democrat Print Co., Madison, WI, 1914.

In addition to published materials, most states have sizable quantities of manuscript and microfilm records of troops. These are especially valuable for the Confederate and border states since the National Archives data tend to be quite incomplete. This is especially true in the case of state and local militia information. Hence, there are listed here such materials for the Confederate and some border states. Please bear in mind that similar materials are often available for the Union states.

___AL: HISTORICAL REFERENCE FILE, AL Department of Archives and History, Montgomery, AL. Look for rosters under the regiment name or number. Also seek deaths, oaths of allegiance, casualties, and substitutes.

___AR: AR CONFEDERATE SERVICE RECORD CARD FILE, alphabetical, AR History Commission, Little Rock, AR.

___FL: FL CIVIL WAR MANUSCRIPT INVENTORY, 3 volumes, FL State Archives, Tallahassee, FL. Look for regimental registers.

___GA: L. Henderson, ROSTER OF THE CONFEDERATE SOLDIERS OF GA, microfilm index, GA Department of Archives and History, Atlanta, GA.

___KY: G. G. Clift, GUIDE TO THE MANUSCRIPTS OF THE KY HISTORICAL SOCIETY, The Society, Frankfort, KY, 1955. Look under Civil War-KY Troops-Confederate.

___LA: RECORDS OF LA CONFEDERATE SOLDIERS AND COMMANDS, microfilm, LA State Library, Baton Rouge, LA.

___MS: NOTEBOOK INVENTORIES TO MS CONFEDERATE RECORDS, MS Department of Archives and History, Jackson, MS. Look under pertinent regiments, paroles, prisoners, deceased soldier claims, petitions, courts-martial.

___MO: CARD INDEX OF MO CONFEDERATE SOLDIERS, only about half listed, Office of the MO Adjutant General, Jefferson City, MO.

___NC: FINDING AIDS NOTEBOOKS: CIVIL WAR COLLECTION FOR NC, NC Department of Archives and History, Raleigh, NC. Look under bounty payrolls, arranged by county.

___SC: RECORDS OF THE SC CONFEDERATE HISTORIAN, SC Department of Archives and History, Columbia, SC. Look at index cards of SC veterans (incomplete) and at 3 volumes of deceased soldiers.

___TN: MANUSCRIPT CARD CATALOG: CIVIL WAR LISTINGS, REGISTER NO. 10-CIVIL WAR COLLECTION, and PAMPHLET LISTING CONTENTS OF RECORD GROUPS, TN State Archives, Nashville, TN. Look under regiments.

___TX: TX MUSTER ROLL CARD INDEX INCLUDING MILITIA, TX Archives Division, Austin, TX.

___VA: CARD INDEX OF VA CONFEDERATE VETERANS, and MILITARY RECORDS GUIDE NOTEBOOK, VA State Archives, Richmond, VA. Look under names, then look under prisoners, names of battles (for those killed), and regiments.

3. State military histories

Many of the states have also published or sponsored the publication of histories of military actions by their

soldiers and sailors.   There are also some histories
dealing with fighting men from particular states which
have been written and published privately.   Both types
will be considered here.   Some of them make numerous
references to individuals, others almost none.   Among
books which you might want to examine are the following:
__AL: W. Brewer, AL, HER HISTORY, RESOURCES, WAR RECORD
AND PUBLIC MEN, 1540-1872, Barrett and Brown, Montgom-
ery, AL, 1872, and J. Wheeler, AL, in Volume 7 of C. E.
Evans, CONFEDERATE MILITARY HISTORY, Confederate Publ.
Co., Atlanta, GA, 1899.
__AR: J. L. Ferguson, AR AND THE CIVIL WAR, Pioneer
Press, Little Rock, AR, 1965, and M. J. Wright, AR IN
THE WAR, Independence County Historical Society, Bates-
ville, AR, 1963, and J. Harrell, AR, in Volume 10 of C.
E. Evans, CONFEDERATE MILITARY HISTORY, Confederate
Publishing Co., Atlanta, GA, 1899.
__CO: J. H. Nankwell, HISTORY OF THE MILITARY ORGANIZA-
TION OF CO, 1860-1935, Kistler Stationery Co., Denver,
CO, 1935.
__CT: CT Adjutant General, CATALOGUE OF CT VOLUNTEER
ORGANIZATIONS IN THE SERVICE OF THE US, 1861-5, Hart-
ford, CT, 1869.
__DE: J. T. Scharf, HISTORY OF DE, 1609-1888, Richards
and Co., Philadelphia, PA, 1888.
__FL: F. L. Robertson, SOLDIERS OF FL IN THE SEMINOLE
INDIAN, CIVIL, AND SPANISH-AMERICAN WARS, Democrat Book
and Job Print, Live Oak, FL, 1909, and J. J. Dickinson,
FL, in Volume 11 of C. E. Evans, CONFEDERATE MILITARY
HISTORY, Confederate Publ. Co., Atlanta, GA, 1899.
__GA: J. T. Derry, GA, in Volume 7 of C. E. Evans, CON-
FEDERATE MILITARY HISTORY, Confederate Publ. Co.,
Atlanta, GA, 1899.
__IN: W. H. H. Terrell, IN ADJUTANT GENERAL'S REPORT,
Conner, Indianapolis, IN, 1865-9.
__IA: L. D. Ingersoll, IA AND THE REBELLION, 1861-5,
Lippincott, Philadelphia, PA, 1867, and A. A. Stuart,
IA COLONELS AND REGIMENTS, Mills and Co., Des Moines,
IA, 1865.
__KS: REPORT OF THE ADJUTANT GENERAL'S OFFICE OF THE
STATE OF KS, 1861-5, KS State Print Co., Topeka, KS,
1867-70, several volumes.
__KY: T. Speed, THE UNION CAUSE IN KY, Putnam's Sons, New
York, NY, 1907, and J. S. Johnstone, KY, in Volume 9 of
C. E. Evans, CONFEDERATE MILITARY HISTORY, Confederate

Publ. Co., Atlanta, GA, 1899; L. H. Harrison, THE CIVIL WAR IN KY, University Press of KY, Lexington, KY, 1982.

LA: A. B. Booth, LA CONFEDERATE MILITARY RECORDS, LA Historical Quarterly 4 (1921), pp. 369-418, and A. B. Booth, RECORDS OF LA CONFEDERATE SOLDIERS AND LA CONFEDERATE COMMANDS, Military Record Commissioner, New Orleans, LA, 1920, and J. B. S. Dimitry, LA, in Volume 10 of C. E. Evans, CONFEDERATE MILITARY HISTORY, Confederate Publ. Co., Atlanta, GA, 1899.

ME: ADJUTANT GENERAL'S ANNUAL REPORTS, 1861-6, Stevens and Sayward, Augusta, ME, 1862-7, 7 volumes, and W. E. S. Whitman and C. H. True, ME IN THE WAR FOR THE UNION, Dingley, Lewiston, ME, 1865.

MD: W. W. Goldsborough, THE MD LINE IN THE CONFEDERATE ARMY, Guggenheimer, Weil, and Co., Baltimore, MD, 1861-5, with INDEX, 1900, Hall of Records Commission Publ. No. 5, Baltimore, MD, 1945, and L. A. Wilmer, HISTORY AND ROSTER OF MD VOLUNTEERS, Guggenheimer, Weil, and Co., Baltimore, MD, 1898-9, 2 volumes, and B. T. Johnson, MD, in Volume 2 of C. E. Evans, CONFEDERATE MILITARY HISTORY, Confederate Publ. Co., Atlanta, GA, 1899.

MA: T. W. Higginson, MA IN THE ARMY & NAVY DURING THE WAR OF 1861-5, Wright and Potter, Boston, MA, 1895-6, and J. L. Bowen, MA IN THE WAR, 1861-5, Springfield, MA, 1889.

MI: J. Robertson, MI IN THE WAR, George and Co., Lansing, MI, 1882.

MN: Board of Commissioners, MN IN THE CIVIL WAR AND INDIAN WARS, 1861-5, Pioneer Press, St. Paul, MN, 1890-3, 2 volumes, with INDEX, MN Historical Society, St. Paul, MN, 1936.

MS: J. C. Rietti, MILITARY ANNALS OF MS, The Author, Jackson, MS, 1895, and D. Rowland, MILITARY HISTORY OF MS IN OFFICIAL AND STATISTICAL REGISTER OF THE STATE OF MS, 1908, pp. 420-943, and C. E. Hooker, MS, in Volume 7 of C. E. Evans, CONFEDERATE MILITARY HISTORY, Confederate Publ. Co., Atlanta, GA, 1889.

MO: US Records and Pension Office, ORGANIZATION AND STATUS OF MO TROOPS IN SERVICE DURING THE CIVIL WAR, Government Printing Office, Washington, DC, 1902, and J. C. Moore, MO, in Volume 9 of C. E. Evans, CONFEDERATE MILITARY HISTORY, Confederate Publ. Co., Atlanta, GA, 1899.

NE: HISTORY OF NE, Western Historical Co., Chicago, IL, 1882, pp. 227-55.

__NH: O. F. R. Waite, NH IN THE GREAT REBELLION CONTAIN-
ING HISTORIES OF THE SEVERAL NH REGIMENTS, 1861-5,
Tracy, Chase, and Co., Claremont, NH, 1870; M. Cleve-
land, NH FIGHTS THE CIVIL WAR, University Press of New
England, Hanover, NH, 1969.
__NJ: J. Y Foster, NJ AND THE REBELLION, Dennis and Co.,
Newark, NJ, 1868, and D. A. Sinclair, THE CIVIL WAR AND
NJ, Centennial Commission, New Brunswick, NJ, 1968.
__NC: W. Clark, HISTORIES OF THE SEVERAL REGIMENTS AND
BATTALIONS FROM NC IN THE GREAT WAR, 1861-5, Nash
Bros., Goldsboro, NC, 1901, and D. H. Hill in Volume 4
of C. E. Evans, CONFEDERATE MILITARY HISTORY, Confed-
erate Publ. Co., Atlanta, GA, 1899, and J. C. Birdsong,
BRIEF SKETCHES OF NC STATE TROOPS IN THE WAR BETWEEN
THE STATES, Daniels, Raleigh, NC, 1894.
__OH: W. Reig, OH IN THE WAR, Moore, Wilstach, and Bald-
win, Cincinnati, OH, 1868.
__SC: E. Capers, SC, in Volume 5 of C. E. Evans, CONFED-
ERATE MILITARY HISTORY, Confederate Publ. Co., Atlanta,
GA, 1899.
__TN: Civil War Centennial Commission, TENNESSEANS IN THE
CIVIL WAR, Mercer, Nashville, TN, 1964, volume 1, and
J. B. Lindsley, THE MILITARY ANNALS OF TN, Reprint Co.,
Spartanburg, SC, 1886 (reprint 1874), and J. D. Porter,
TN, in Volume 8, CONFEDERATE MILITARY HISTORY, Confed-
erate Publ. Co., Atlanta, GA, 1899.
__TX: O. M. Roberts, TX, in volume 11 of C. E. Evans,
CONFEDERATE MILITARY HISTORY, Confederate Publ. Co.,
Atlanta, GA, 1899, and L. N. Fitzhugh, TX BATTERIES,
BATTALIONS, REGIMENTS, COMMANDERS, AND FIELD OFFICERS,
Mirror Press, Midlothian, TX, 1959, and M. J. Wright,
TX IN THE WAR, 1861-5, Hill Jr. College Press, Hills-
boro, TX, 1965.
__VT: G. G. Benedict, VT IN THE CIVIL WAR, Free Press,
Burlington, VT, 1886-8.
__VA: L. A. Wallace, A GUIDE TO VA MILITARY ORGANIZA-
TIONS, 1861-5, VA Civil War Commission, Richmond, VA,
1964, and J. Hotchkiss, VA, in Volume 3 of C. E. Evans,
CONFEDERATE MILITARY HISTORY, Confederate Publ. Co.,
Atlanta, GA, 1899.
__WV: T. F. Lang, LOYAL WV FROM 1861 TO 1865, Deutsch
Publ. Co., Baltimore, MD, 1895, and R. White, WV, in
Volume 2 of C. E. Evans, CONFEDERATE MILITARY HISTORY,
Confederate Publ. Co., Atlanta, GA, 1899.
__WI: W. D. Love, WI IN THE WAR OF THE REBELLION, Church
and Goodman, Chicago, IL, 1866, and E. B. Quiner, THE

MILITARY HISTORY OF WI, Clarke and Co., Chicago, IL, 1866.

Many other volumes on histories of military units in the Civil War will be given in Chapter 6 which is entitled MILITARY UNIT HISTORIES.

4. Confederate pension lists

As you will recall from previous sections, pensions were not awarded to Confederates by the US Federal government. However, pensions were given to them by the Confederate states and by some of the border states which had sizable Confederate enlistees (such as KY). The dates on which these states began issuing pensions are: AL(1867), AR(1891), FL(1885), GA(1870), KY(1902), LA(1898), MS(1888), MO(1913), NC(1885), OK(1915), SC(1898), TN(1891), TX(1881), VA(1888). Early on, Confederate pensions were usually restricted to veterans who were totally disabled. Then as time went on, they were opened up to indigent veterans and indigent widows, then finally, to all veterans and all widows. A few pension application indexes have been published. Others are available in card, manuscript, or microfilm form, mostly in State Archives. Included are:

CONFEDERATE PENSION FILES ARRANGED BY COUNTY, AL Department of Archives and History, Montgomery, AL.

F. T. Ingmire, AR CONFEDERATE VETERANS' AND WIDOWS' PENSION APPLICATIONS, Ingmire Publishing, St. Louis, MO, 1985.

FL Comptroller's Office, REPORT OF THE COMPTROLLER OF FL, 1882-1906, The Comptroller, Tallahassee, FL, 1882-1906. [Lists Confederate pensioners].

MICROFILM INDEX TO GA CONFEDERATE PENSION APPLICATIONS, GA Department of Archives and History, Atlanta, GA.

M. L. Cook, KY CONFEDERATE VETERAN AND WIDOW PENSION INDEX, Cook Publications, Evansville, IN, 1979.

A. Simpson, CONFEDERATE PENSION APPLICATIONS OF KY, KY Division of Archives and Records Management, Frankfort, KY, 1980.

INDEX TO LA CONFEDERATE PENSION FILES, State Archives and Records Service, Baton Rouge, LA.

MS CONFEDERATE PENSION APPLICATIONS, in alphabetical order, MS Department of Archives and History, Jackson, MS.

__MO CONFEDERATE PENSION APPLICATIONS, in alphabetical order, Office of the MO Adjutant General, Jefferson City, MO.

__NOTEBOOK INDEXES TO NC CONFEDERATE PENSION APPLICATIONS, be sure to examine each of the 2 notebooks, NC Department of Archives and History, Raleigh, NC.

__INDEX TO OK CONFEDERATE PENSION APPLICATIONS, OK Genealogical Society, Oklahoma City, OK, 1969.

__SC CONFEDERATE PENSION APPLICATIONS, arranged by county, and SC CONFEDERATE PENSION APPLICATIONS INDEX, 1919-25, computer printout, SC Department of Archives and History, Columbia, SC.

__TN State Library and Archives, INDEX TO TN CONFEDERATE PENSION APPLICATIONS, The Library and Archives, Nashville, TN, 1964.

__J. M. Kinney and P. Oakley, INDEX TO APPLICATIONS FOR TX CONFEDERATE PENSIONS, TX State Library, Austin, TX, 1980.

__MICROFILM INDEX TO VA CONFEDERATE PENSION APPLICATIONS, VA State Archives, Richmond, VA.

5. State biographies

If your Civil War ancestor had a degree of prominence in state politics, business, large-scale farming, banking, or the professions (law, teaching, medicine, religion), it is possible that there will be a biographical sketch of him in a state biographical collection or compendium. Many of these volumes were published in the years after the War, and if you can locate his biography in one of them, the sketch will undoubtedly contain some details on his military career.

A sizable number of state biographical compendiums can be located by looking under the pertinent state in the reference volumes:

__P. W. Filby, AMERICAN & BRITISH GENEALOGY & HERALDRY, New England Historic Genealogical Society, Boston, MA, 1983, with SUPPLEMENTS, to date.

If something is found there, the biographical book may be borrowed on interlibrary loan. It might also be well to send an SASE and an inquiry to the state archives asking them what biographical collections they have available. Addresses of these archives appear in section 3 of Chapter 2.

Chapter 5

LOCAL SOURCES

1. Introduction

In addition to national and state sources of Civil
War personnel records, there are a sizable number of
sources available at the county and city levels. These
consist of family Bible records, cemetery records, gravestone inscriptions, church records, city histories,
county histories, court records, genealogical periodical
articles, genealogical societies, historical societies,
marriage anniversary accounts, mortuary records, newspaper obituaries, and published genealogies. These and
many other possible sources of genealogical information
on your Civil War ancestor are treated in detail with
precise instructions for searching in:
_Geo. K. Schweitzer, GENEALOGICAL SOURCE HANDBOOK,
available from the author at the address on the title
page of this book.

In the sections to follow some of the better possi-
bilities from among the above local sources will be discussed in detail. It is important to check the cities
and counties where your ancestor lived when he enlisted,
and the cities and counties where he lived and died after
the Civil War was over.

2. Place of enlistment

If you know the city and/or county where your Civil
War veteran enlisted, there are a number of searches you
can make in order to find records. The first inquiry
should take place within your family to see if anyone
knows of records which were kept in a family Bible or
prayer book. The most usual things to be recorded were
birth, marriage, and death dates, but sometimes Civil War
service enlistments were entered. Then inquire within
your family as to whether anyone has any old official
papers or war items which originally belonged to your ancestor.

The second approach you should make is to look for
city and/or county history books, especially ones which
were published between 1865 and 1900. These often car-

ried details of military units raised in their area along
with rosters of men who served from the locality. To
locate such histories, consult:

__M. J. Kaminkow, US LOCAL HISTORIES IN THE LIBRARY OF
  CONGRESS, Magna Carta Book Co., Baltimore, MD, 1975, 5
  volumes, plus SUPPLEMENTS.
__P. W. Filby, A BIBLIOGRAPHY OF AMERICAN COUNTY HIS-
  TORIES, Genealogical Publishing Co., Baltimore, MD,
  1985.

Once you have located pertinent volumes, you may have
them borrowed for you through interlibrary loan (see
section 1 of Chapter 3).

Then, thirdly, you can dispatch an SASE to the
county clerk to ask if any Civil War enlistee records
were kept. The addresses of these clerks may be obtained
from:

__G. B. Everton, Sr., HANDY BOOK FOR GENEALOGISTS, Ever-
  ton Publishers, Logan, UT, latest issue.

As a fourth action to take, letters of inquiry along
with SASEs should be addressed to the local genealogical
society, the local historical society, and the local
library asking if records of Civil War enlistees from the
area are available. Addresses of local genealogical
societies may be obtained from:

__M. K. Meyer, DIRECTORY OF GENEALOGICAL SOCIETIES IN THE
  USA, The Author, Pasadena, MD, latest edition.
__J. Konrad, GENEALOGICAL AND HISTORICAL SOCIETIES,
  Summit Publications, Munroe Falls, OH, latest edition.
__V. N. Chambers, editor, THE GENEALOGICAL HELPER,
  Everton Publishers, Logan, UT, latest Jul-Aug issue.

Addresses of local historical societies will be found in
the volume just mentioned by Konrad and in:

__DIRECTORY: HISTORICAL SOCIETIES AND AGENCIES IN THE US
  AND CANADA, Nashville, TN, latest edition.

And addresses of local libraries are obtainable in:

__AMERICAN LIBRARY DIRECTORY, Bowker, New York, NY,
  latest issue.

3. Place of residence

With a knowledge of the city and/or county where
your veteran lived after the War, you can pursue your
record search even further. The first approach you
should make is to send letters with SASEs to the local

library, the local historical society, and the local
genealogical society asking them two things: (a) if there
are newspaper records of marriage anniversaries of your
veteran and his wife, and (b) if there are membership
records for local branches of Civil War veterans'
organizations such as the Grand Army of the Republic,
Union Veterans' Legion, Union Veterans' Union, United
Confederate Veterans, or United Sons of Confederate
Veterans. Addresses of the local institutions may be
obtained by using the reference volumes listed in section
2 of this chapter.

Then, secondly, you should attempt to find city
and/or county histories. These volumes, especially those
written between 1865 and 1900 often carried biographical
sketches of citizens of the area. Inevitably if the
citizen was a Civil War veteran, his sketch would refer
to his military service, usually in considerable detail.
History works of this type may be discovered in the
volumes by Kaminkow and Filby which were mentioned in the
second item of the previous section (section 2). Once
discovered, you may obtain the books through interlibrary
loan.

4. Place of death

Knowing the exact or approximate date of death of
your Civil War ancestor, there are numerous routes to
explore for information concerning him. First, check
with your family concerning the existence of family Bible
or prayer book records. It is possible that your ancestor's death date in the record may carry a notation about
military service, especially if he died in the War.

Second, address an inquiry accompanied by an SASE
and a check for $4 to the caretaker of the cemetery in
which your ancestor is buried. Ask if there are any
detailed records on those who have been buried there, and
if so, whether there is anything about your ancestor's
Civil War record. If you have not seen the gravestone,
also ask for a copy or a picture of the inscription,
since these inscriptions often carried notations on the
military unit.

Third, if you know or suspect what mortuary handled
your veteran's funeral service, send them an SASE and ask

for any records they may be able to supply you with.
Quite often the name of the mortuary will appear on the
death certificate. Names and addresses of mortuaries may
be found in:
__C. O. Kates, editor, THE AMERICAN BLUE BOOK FOR FUNERAL
  DIRECTORS, Kates-Boylston Publications, New York, NY,
  latest issue.
__NATIONAL DIRECTORY OF MORTICIANS, National Directory of
  Morticians, Youngstown, OH, latest issue.
Almost all mortuaries have copies of one or both of
these.

     For the <u>fourth</u> approach, address inquiries and send
SASEs to the local library, the local genealogical society, and the local historical society asking them for two
items: (a) newspaper obituaries of your ancestor, and (b)
whether they might have records which veterans' organizations (such as mentioned under the 1st item of section 3
of this chapter) may have kept of the funeral service
which they conducted for the veteran. Addresses of the
libraries and societies will be found in the books mentioned in the 4th item of section 2 of this chapter.

Chapter 6

MILITARY UNIT HISTORIES

1. Tracking war experiences

In a sense, the previous chapter (state rosters and regimental histories) has introduced you to the possibility of tracing your Civil War ancestor through his wartime experiences. Fortunately, the abundance of records makes it possible for most veterans to be traced in a quite detailed fashion. It is fascinating to follow your ancestor practically on a day-to-day basis through his war service. This may usually be done by examining histories of his military unit (regiment in the army or ship in the navy). Some insight to such histories has been given in Chapter 4 (state publications: regimental histories). In addition to this, there are numerous other sources of military unit histories which will now be discussed.

2. Field records .

The official field records of the Civil War referred to in Chapter 3 (section 2) may be used to find a large number of on-the-scene reports relating to battle operations of many Union and Confederate army regiments and naval ships. You will recall that there are 128 volumes of army records and 31 volumes of naval records.

To look up your ancestor's army regiment, employ the index to the 128-volumed set of army records:
  Index, OFFICIAL RECORDS OF THE UNION AND CONFEDERATE ARMIES IN THE WAR OF THE REBELLION, Government Printing Office, Washington, DC, 1901.
Turn to the state and then find the designation Troops followed by (C.) or by (U.), indicating Confederate or Union. For example, if your ancestor served in the 3rd TN Infantry on the Union side, look for Tennessee Troops (U.). Under this heading you will discover the various regiments, including the 3rd Infantry, listed along with references to their military activities.

To look up your ancestor's naval ship use the index to the 31-volumed set of naval records:

__Index, OFFICIAL RECORDS OF THE UNION AND CONFEDERATE
NAVIES IN THE WAR OF THE REBELLION, Government Printing
Office, Washington, DC, 1922.
Simply find the name of the ship, Union or Confederate,
and beneath its listing will appear the references to the
pertinent documents. The naval records, surprisingly,
also contain numerous references to army regiments, so do
not fail to look for your ancestor's army regiment in
this index also.

3. National Archives

The National Archives in Washington has a vast
number of documents relating to the military ventures of
army regiments, navy ships, naval stations, and specific
battles and military encounters. If you wish to explore
these write the following address:
__Military Service Records (NNCC), National Archives,
GSS, Washington, DC 20408.
Ask them to send you a list of records on your ancestor's
regiment, ship, station, or a military action in which he
was involved, along with costs for photocopying or for
purchasing microfilms if they are available. It may take
quite some time for your reply to come, but as often as
not, the wait will be worth it.

4. Reference volumes

There is a very important set of reference volumes
which will lead you to printed regimental histories on
your ancestor's regiment. This set is known as:
__C. E. Dornbusch, MILITARY BIBLIOGRAPHY OF THE CIVIL
WAR, NY Public Library, New York, NY, 1961-72, 3 volumes.
All you need to do is look for your ancestor's state,
then under the state you will find his regiment listed.
The infantry, cavalry, artillery, and engineers are shown
separately. Under each regiment you will find references
to books, pamphlets, and journal articles chronicling the
history of the regiment or some portion of it. Associated with many references is a set of abbreviations
(such as CSmH, DLC, TxU, NN, or Vi). These indicate the
names of libraries in which Dornbusch knows the references can be found. Your librarian can provide you with
the key to these abbreviations which are listed in:

___SYMBOLS OF AMERICAN LIBRARIES, Library of Congress,
Washington, DC, latest edition.
The abbreviations do not indicate that these are the only
libraries in which the various volumes are to be found.
Many of the books are the property of numerous libraries.

Once a book on your ancestor's regiment has been
found in Dornbusch's reference set, it is wise for you to
look that book up in the following 2-volumed work:
___A. Nevins, J. I. Robertson, Jr., and B. I. Wiley, CIVIL
WAR BOOKS: A CRITICAL BIBLIOGRAPHY, LA State University
Press, Baton Rouge, LA, 1967.
The books list many Civil War publications and then give
you a brief critical evaluation of each, especially
whether it is accurate. This information will assist you
in deciding whether you think it worth your expense and
time to borrow it on interlibrary loan.

Should you desire to follow the history of your
naval veteran ancestor, consult:
___M. J. Smith, Jr., AMERICAN CIVIL WAR NAVIES, Scarecrow
Press, Metuchen, NJ, 1972.
This work is quite similar to Dornbusch and will provide
references, if any are available, for your further in-
vestigation. Almost 3000 entries are given. Three other
compilations of thousands of Civil War volumes which
should be consulted in your quest for materials relating
to your ancestor's military unit or ship are:
___T. Broadfoot, CIVIL WAR BOOKS: A PRICED CHECKLIST,
Broadfoot's Bookmark, Wendell, NC, 1980.
___R. Harwell, CONFEDERATE PUBLICATIONS, Broadfoot's
Bookmark, Wendell, NC, 1982.
___M. Mullins and R. Reed, THE UNION BOOKSHELF, Broad-
foot's Bookmark, Wendell, NC, 1982.

There are occasions in which you will not know the
official state and number of a Civil War participant's
regiment. Instead you may have only a name, such as
Bells Babies, All Saints' Riflemen, Lafayette Farmers,
Abe's Rejecters, St. Peter's Guards, Manitowoc Guards, or
Bath City Grays. To ascertain what the official states
and numbers of the regiments or parts of regiments were
you need to use two volumes which identify names of this
sort. For Union and Confederate army military unit
names, employ:

__W. Amann, PERSONNEL OF THE CIVIL WAR, Yoseloff, New
York, NY, 1961.

For Confederate army military units, you may use in
addition:

__W. Tancig, CONFEDERATE MILITARY LAND UNITS, Yoseloff,
New York, NY, 1969.

Incidentally, Abe's Rejecters were Company B of the 41st
MS Infantry.

5. Compendiums

There are two large collections of Civil War regimental histories. The first of these is:

__F. H. Dyer, A COMPENDIUM OF THE WAR OF THE REBELLION,
Yoseloff, New York, NY, 1908 (reprint 1959), 3 volumes.

Listed in these excellent volumes are well over 2000
Union regimental histories. Another collection of regimental histories is:

__THE UNION ARMY: A HISTORY OF MILITARY AFFAIRS IN THE
LOYAL STATES, 1861-5, Federal Publ. Co., Madison, WI
1908, 8 volumes, the 1st four being regimental histories and the 7th on the navy.

Please recall that section 3 of Chapter 4 (state military
histories) lists numerous sources of regimental histories
published for individual states.

6. Maps

As you make your way through the historical events
of your Civil War ancestor's life in the military service, it will often be of help to you to visualize certain events (particularly battles, troop movements, and
ship journeys) on appropriate maps. There are several
very good atlases available for your assistance. Notable
among them is the official atlas designed to accompany
the official field reports:

__C. O. Cowles, THE OFFICIAL ATLAS OF THE CIVIL WAR,
Yoseloff, New York, NY, 1891-5 (reprint 1958).

In addition, the following volume is as good, if not
better, than the official atlas:

__V. J. Esposito, THE WEST POINT ATLAS OF AMERICAN WARS,
Praeger, New York, NY, 1951, Volume 1, pp. xii-xiii,
maps 17-154.

Also to be recommended, not only for its maps, but for
its well-done panoramic views of battlefields is:

H. H. Kagan, THE AMERICAN HERITAGE PICTORIAL ATLAS OF
US HISTORY, American Heritage, New York, NY, 1966, pp.
194-241.

In addition to the maps gathered together in atlases, there are thousands of detailed local-region maps
which have been collected by the Map Division of the
Library of Congress and by the National Archives. These
maps show troop positions and movements, battle lines,
and fortifications. Over 8000 maps are listed in these
three volumes:

R. W. Stephenson, CIVIL WAR MAPS, Library of Congress,
Washington, DC, 1961.

CIVIL WAR MAPS IN THE NATIONAL ARCHIVES, National Archives and Records Service, Washington, DC, 1964.

C. E. LeGear, THE HOTCHKISS MAP COLLECTION, Library of
Congress, Washington, DC, 1951.

The first two volumes contain maps, most of which were
prepared by Federal authorities. The last volume, however, lists a large number of Confederate maps. Photodup-
licated copies of maps listed in these books may be
obtained from the agencies which published the volumes.

Photoduplication Service, Library of Congress, 10 First
St., Washington, DC 20540.

National Archives and Records Service, PA Ave. between
7th and 9th Sts., Washington, DC 20408.

7. US Army Military History Institute

An important source for military unit historical
material is the US Army Military History Institute, which
is located at Carlisle Barracks, PA. This institute is
the Army's official central repository for historical
source materials of the US Army. The Civil War is very
well represented in its 300,000 books, 30,000 bound
volumes of periodicals, 9300 boxes of manuscripts, thousands of photographs, and numerous other documents. Among
these holdings are the 19th Century US War Department
Library, troop rosters (usually unindexed) published by
various state Adjutants General, personal papers (diaries, letters, records) of hundreds of officers and enlisted men, regimental histories, regimental and individual photographs, and many pieces of military art and
artifacts. This very large collection pertains to soldiers of various designations: regulars, volunteers, and
militia.

In order to avail yourself of the Institute's vast holdings, you need to know your ancestor's military unit, since the Institute has no master index of soldiers. If you know the military unit, send the Institute an SASE, your ancestor's name, and his military unit, and ask them to see what they can find pertaining to the soldier's unit. The address is:

__Reference Branch, The US Army Military History Institute, Carlisle Barracks, PA 17013.

They may be able to provide you with a published history of the unit, unpublished letters and/or diaries of some of its soldiers, roster references to your soldier, photographs of the unit, perhaps even of your ancestor. In addition to materials relating to your soldier's regiment, there may also be available materials relating to other regiments in the same brigade, as well as brigade records. The staff of the Institute cannot do extensive research, but they will locate for you pertinent materials in their collection. If research and/or copying is called for, you will need to employ a professional researcher or visit the Institute yourself. The Institute is open 8:00 am-4:30 pm, Mondays through Fridays, except Federal holidays.

8. Other sources

A number of specialized categories are represented in the volumes by Nevins, Robertson, and Wiley (see section 4 in this chapter). Among those you may be interested in because they may be relevant to your ancestor's military career are:

__PRISONS AND PRISONERS OF WAR, Volume 1, pp. 185-206.
__THE NEGRO, Volume 1, pp. 207-216.
__THE NAVIES, Volume 1, pp. 217-239.

There are also a number of special sections in the volumes by Dornbusch (see section 4 of this chapter) which could prove to be very helpful to you:

__CEMETERIES, Volume 3, pp. 6-7.
__ETHNIC GROUPS, Volume 3, pp. 11-3.
__INDIANS, Volume 3, p. 22.
__NEGROES, Volume 3, pp. 24-5.
__PRISONS AND PRISONERS OF WAR, Volume 3, pp. 43-50.
__VETERANS AND THEIR ORGANIZATIONS, Volume 3, pp. 52-56.

As you trace your Civil War soldier through the War, you will probably find it helpful to use a day-by-day

listing of the major events of the conflict. Two very
useful accounts of this sort are available. The first
one is:

__E. B.   and B. Long, THE CIVIL WAR DAY BY DAY, Doubleday
and Co., New York, NY, 1971.

This book treats the war chronologically giving you the
events that occurred on each day, presenting a brief
summary of each event.   Major occurrences appear in
capitals. Another useful day-by-day set of accounts will
be found in:

__F. H. Dyer, A COMPENDIUM OF THE WAR OF THE REBELLION,
Morningside Bookshop Press, Dayton, OH, Volume 2.

This book has an index of campaigns, battles, engage-
ments, actions, combats, sieges, skirmishes, and other
military events (pp. 595-659). The index will refer you
to the state or territory in which the event happened and
the date.   You can then turn to the state or territory
involved and under it you will find a chronological
listing which will contain the event you are interested
in.   After it will be shown the Federal troops (regiments, battalions, batteries) which took part.   The book
also gives a regimental index which shows the larger
units to which each regiment, battalion, or battery was
attached (brigades, divisions, corps, armies).

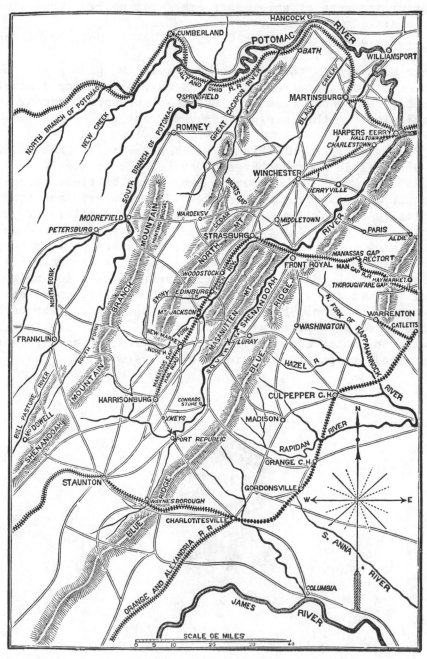

THE SHENANDOAH VALLEY

Chapter 7

CIVIL WAR EVENTS, RELICS, SITES, & MEMORIES

1. Introduction

In the process of delving deeper and deeper into your Civil War ancestor's military career, you are likely to accumulate a great deal of information. Many of these data may deal with places your ancestor was (cities, towns, areas, camp sites, battle fields, river crossings, railroad centers, harbors). Other data will probably cause you to wonder about the uniforms he wore, the weapons he used, the equipment he carried, the tents he camped in, the cities he attacked or retreated from, the food he ate, the hospitals he was treated in, the prisons he was held in, the earthworks from behind which he fought, how he and his companions entertained themselves, and whether photographs were taken of him. There are many relics (or remains) of the Civil War which will permit you to continue your investigations into these aspects of your veteran's military service. We will examine various relics (records, photographs, historic sites, museum collections, patriotic societies) which you may want to pursue in quest of the surroundings of your Union or Confederate ancestor's military years.

2. Libraries

In many of the states of the US you will find at least one library which has a good to excellent collection of Civil War books, documents, and microfilms. If your interest warrants it, you may plan to visit one or more of these libraries. Ask the librarian to assist you in examining the card catalog for materials dealing with the subjects you are interested in. Also do not fail to go into the stacks and simply take a look at the books on the shelves and the labels on the microfilm cartons. In addition, you must not forget to ask if the librarian has a special section in which old Civil War books and documents are housed.

It is well to bear in mind that even though any of the good Civil War libraries will be of assistance to you, the libraries nearer the places where your ancestor was involved are more likely to have pertinent informa-

tion.   Names and locations of libraries with good to excellent Civil War collections are given in:
__M. L. and H. C. Young, DIRECTORY OF SPECIAL LIBRARIES, Gale Research Co., Detroit, MI, 1979, see index on page 1236.
__L. Ash, SUBJECT COLLECTIONS, Bowker, New York, NY, 1978, pp. 1109-1112.
If Civil War records you have found indicate that your ancestor took part in a military action in or near a city, it is quite possible that the library in that city will have records of the event.   If the military action was in or near a village or a town, it is less likely that there will be local records, but it is a mistake not to inquire.   Names and addresses of libraries in these cities, towns, and villages will be found in:
__AMERICAN LIBRARY DIRECTORY, Bowker, New York, NY, latest issue.
Before travelling to visit any library, be sure and send them an SASE and an inquiry concerning whether they have records which might help you and the times when they are open.

3. Historic sites

    Many organizations, both governmental and private, have identified, marked, preserved, beautified, and/or restored numerous historical sites associated with the Civil War.   A great deal of enjoyment can be had by visiting those with which your Civil War ancestor was affiliated.   In conjunction with most of these places there are often libraries and/or museums. They are very valuable; don't overlook them.

    The most elaborate of the Civil War historical site installations are the Civil War areas under the super-vision of the National Park Service. Among these are:
__ANTIETAM NATIONAL BATTLEFIELD SITE & CEMETERY, PO Box 158, Sharpsburg, MD 21782.
__APPOMATTOX COURT HOUSE NATIONAL HISTORICAL PARK, PO Box 218, Appomattox, VA 24522.
__BRICES CROSSROADS NATIONAL BATTLEFIELD SITE, Superin-tendent, Natchez Trace Parkway, RR 1, NT-143, Tupelo, MS 33801.
__CHICKAMAUGA AND CHATTANOOGA NATIONAL MILITARY PARK, PO Box 2126, Fort Oglethorpe, GA 30742.

___FORT DONELSON NATIONAL MILITARY PARK, Box F, Dover, TN 37058.

___FREDERICKSBURG AND SPOTSYLVANIA COUNTY BATTLEFIELD MEMORIAL NATIONAL MILITARY PARK AND CEMETERY, PO Box 679, Fredericksburg, VA 22401.

___GETTYSBURG NATIONAL MILITARY PARK AND CEMETERY, PO Box 70, Gettysburg, PA 17325.

___HARPERS FERRY NATIONAL HISTORICAL PARK, PO Box 65, Harpers Ferry, WV 25425.

___KENNESAW MOUNTAIN NATIONAL BATTLEFIELD PARK, PO Box 1167, Marietta, GA 30061.

___MANASSAS NATIONAL BATTLEFIELD PARK, PO Box 350, Manassas, VA 22110.

___PEA RIDGE NATIONAL MILITARY PARK, Pea Ridge, AR 72751.

___PETERSBURG NATIONAL BATTLEFIELD, PO Box 549, Petersburg, VA 23803.

___RICHMOND NATIONAL BATTLEFIELD PARK, 3215 East Broad St., Richmond, VA 23223.

___SHILOH NATIONAL MILITARY PARK AND CEMETERY, Shiloh, TN 38376.

___STONES RIVER NATIONAL BATTLEFIELD AND CEMETERY, PO Box 1039, Murfreesboro, TN 37130.

___TUPELO NATIONAL BATTLEFIELD, Superintendent, Natchez Trace Parkway, RR 1, NT-143, Tupelo, MS 38801.

___VICKSBURG NATIONAL MILITARY PARK AND CEMETERY, PO Box 349, Vicksburg, MS 39180.

___WILSON'S CREEK NATIONAL BATTLEFIELD, Route 2, Box 75, Republic, MO 65738.

Addresses have been supplied so that you can write and ask for a descriptive pamphlet before making a visit.

In addition to these very large sites, there are hundreds more, some small, some large, ranging all the way from the old Federal Armory (Union troop headquarters) in Copperopolis, CA, to the Civil War cannons in Fort Allen Park at Portland, ME, and from Fort Taylor in Key West, FL, to the Civil War Veterans' Monument in Ottumwa, IA. If you do any travelling at all in the pursuit of your Civil War interests, there is a book which is a necessity. This volume is:

___A H. Cromie, A TOUR GUIDE TO THE CIVIL WAR, Dutton, New York, NY, 1975.

In it there are described Civil War cemeteries, parks, forts, battle sites, buildings, libraries, memorials, houses, statues, churches, markers, and museums in and/or near well over 2000 cities, towns, villages, and counties

all over the US.   Accompanying each is a brief descrip-
tion, and often a history of the event memorialized.
Another book which is similar is:

__E. Fodor, FODOR'S CIVIL WAR SITES, McKay, New York, NY,
__1979.

These books will serve as very effective guides as you
search out the sites and events of your Civil War ancestor's military service. Two other notable volumes which
may be of interest to you are composed of hundreds of
listings, comments, and pictures of Confederate and Union
Civil War monuments:

__R. W. Widener, CONFEDERATE MONUMENTS, The Author,
__Dallas, TX, 1981.
__Daughters of Union Veterans, CIVIL WAR UNION MONUMENTS,
__The Daughters, Washington, DC, 1982.

4. Museums and panoramas

As you might imagine, there are many museums which
have displays of Civil War materials, and there are a
sizable number which are devoted entirely to the Civil
War. Here you will see weapons, uniforms, flags, insignia, camp furniture, cannons, vehicles, equipment, documents, saddles, and many other types of relics.   There
are also in a few places three-dimensional panoramic
models of battles, some of them quite elaborate.

In addition to the museums and panoramas associated
with the historic sites mentioned in the previous section
(see section 3), the following are among others worth a
visit:

__AL: Museum of Mobile in Mobile, White House of Con-
__federacy in Montgomery, State Archives in Montgomery.
__AR:Fort Museum in Fort Smith, also see section 3 above.
__CA: Lincoln Shrine in Redlands, Fort Point in San
__Francisco.
__DE: Fort Delaware in Delaware City.
__DC: American Red Cross, Lincoln Museum, Smithsonian
__Institution, and US Naval Museum, all in Washington.
__FL: South FL Museum in Bradenton, Olustee Battlefield
__Museum in Olustee.
__GA: Atlanta Historical Society and Cyclorama in Atlan-
__ta, Confederate Museum in Irwinville, Battlerama and
__Big Shanty Museum in Kennesaw, and Stone Mountain
__Museum in DeKalb County, also see section 3 above.

__IL: Chicago Historical Society in Chicago, Galena Historical Museum in Galena, Quincy Historical Society in Quincy, Lincoln Museum in Springfield.

__KY: Columbus-Belmont Battlefield Museum in Columbus, KY Military History Museum in Frankfort, and Perryville Battlefield Museum and Diorama in Boyle County.

__LA: Lafayette Museum in Lafayette, Mansfield Battle Museum in Mansfield, Chalmette National Historical Park in Arabi, Confederate Museum in New Orleans, and LA State Exhibit Museum in Shreveport.

__ME: GAR Hall in Bath.

__MD: Naval Academy Museum in Annapolis, and Maryland Historical Society in Baltimore, also section 3 above.

__MA : Historical Museum of the North and South in Acton, and First Corps Cadet Armory in Boston.

__MI: Cass County Pioneer Museum in Cassopolis, Henry Ford Museum in Dearborn, Detroit Historical Museum and Fort Wayne Military Museum in Detroit, Grand Rapids Public Museum in Grand Rapids, Kalamazoo Public Museum in Kalamazoo.

__MS: Old South Museum in Beauvoir, Grand Gulf Military Park Museum near Port Gibson, MS State Historical Museum in Jackson, Russell Memorial in Port Gibson, and Old Court House Museum in Vicksburg, also see section 3 above.

__MO: Jackson County Museum in Independence, State Museum in Jefferson City, Kansas City Museum in Kansas City, Lone Jack Museum and Diorama in Lone Jack, and Jefferson Barracks Museum just south of St. Louis, also see section 3 above.

__NE: Fort Kearney Museum in Kearney County, and State Historical Society Museum in Lincoln.

__NM: Fort Union Museum in Watrous.

__NY: NY State Museum in Albany, Fort Ontario at Oswego, and West Point Museum in West Point.

__NC: Hall of History in Raleigh, and Fort Branch Museum in Williamston.

__OH: Hamilton County Memorial Building in Cincinnati, OH History Center in Columbus, Hayes State Memorial in Fremont.

__OK: Fort Gibson in Fort Gibson.

__PA: War Library and Museum of The Military Order of The Loyal Legion of the US in Philadelphia, and Allegheny County Soldiers and Sailors Memorial Hall in Pittsburgh, also see section 3 above.

__RI: Newport Artillery Company Armory in Newport.

__SC: Confederate Park Museum in Aiken, Confederate Museum and Hunley Museum in Charleston, State Archives in Columbia, Fort Sumter on Sullivan's Island in Charleston Harbor, The Carolina Museum in Lancaster.

__TN: Confederama and Lookout Mountain Museum in Chattanooga, Cumberland Gap in Claiborne County, and Children's Museum in Nashville, also see section 3 above.

__TX: Daughters of the Confederacy Museum in Austin, Fort Belknap Museum in Newcastle, Fort Davis Museum in Fort Davis, and Confederate Research Center in Hillsboro.

__VT: State Historical Society in Montpelier and Norwich University Museum in Northfield.

__VA: Fort Monroe in Fort Monroe, Warren Rifles Museum in Front Royal, Chapel at Washington and Lee University in Lexington, New Market Battlefield Park at New Market, Army Transport Museum and Mariners Museum in Petersburg, Naval Shipyard Museum in Portsmouth, and Confederate Museum in Richmond, also see section 3 above.

__WV: Civil War Showcase in Harpers Ferry, also see section 3 above.

__WI: GAR Memorial Hall in State Capitol in Madison.

5. Patriotic organizations

Shortly after the Civil War, veterans of both sides began organizing to form patriotic societies to promote social activities, war record preservation, and veterans' interests. The first of these organizations to form was the Military Order of the Loyal Legion of the US (abbreviated MOLLUS). It was organized in 1865 and was open to former Union commissioned officers, their male descendants, and civilians who gave distinguished service to the Union. At the turn of the century there were twenty state commanderies: PA, NY, ME, MA, CA, WI, IL, DC, OH, MI, MN, OR, MO, NE, KS, IA , CO, IN, WA, and VT, listed in the order of seniority. The largest such society was the Grand Army of the Republic (GAR). It was organized in 1866 and was open to all Union veterans. The society consisted of state departments which in turn were subdivided into almost 6000 local camps. The membership rose to a maximum of about 409,000 in 1890, then steadily declined. Two similar organizations, the Union Veteran Legion and the Union Veteran Union, were organized in 1884 and 1886. Their membership requirements were more restrictive than those of the GAR, about 20,000 and 70,000 members belonging to them in 1900. There were also organizations representing smaller units, such as those of particular Civil War armies (Potomac, Cumberland, TN), particular brigades, particular regiments, and particular companies. There was also a National Association of Naval Veterans. In the Southern states, the largest comparable society was the United Confederate Veterans (UCV). It was organized in 1889 with an object of preserving War data, aiding veterans and their families, memorializing the dead, and keeping war friendships alive. It was open to all Confederate veterans. As of the turn of the century there were over 65,000 members organized into nearly 1500 local camps within three departments (the armies of Northern VA, TN, and trans--MS). Its official publication was the magazine THE CONFEDERATE VETERAN referred to in section 7 of Chapter 3.

As time went on, these organizations gave rise to auxiliaries and separate societies for descendants of veterans. In the North, the GAR established two auxiliary organizations, the Women's Relief Corps (for wives, daughters, and sisters), and the Sons of Veterans (for male descendants). In the South, there were organized the United Sons of Confederate Veterans (for male descendants) and United Daughters of the Confederacy (for widows, wives, mothers, sisters, and female descendants). Many other such societies came into being.

At the present time, the GAR has disbanded, its national records being turned over to the Library of Congress and its insignia to the Smithsonian Institution in 1956. MOLLUS survives and maintains a Civil War library of 10,000 volumes plus a museum:
　MOLLUS War Library and Museum, 1805 Pine St., Philadelphia, PA 19103.
Its many previous publications are referenced in the work by Dornbusch (see section 4 of Chapter 6). The National Women's Corps of the GAR (18,000 members) has 29 state and 830 local groups and maintains a GAR Memorial Museum.
　National Women's Relief Corps, Auxiliary to the GAR, 629 S. Seventh St., Springfield, IL 62703.
The Daughters of Union Veterans (15,000 members) conduct genealogical work and maintain records and a library.
　Daughters of Union Veterans, 503 S. Walnut St., Springfield, IL 62704.

The United Daughters of the Confederacy (35,000 members) maintain a 2500-volume library and share quarters with their affiliate organization Children of the Confederacy (10,000 members).
__United Daughters of the Confederacy and Children of the Confederacy, 328 North Blvd., Richmond, VA 23220.
The Sons of Confederate Veterans maintains a small library of Confederate materials.
__Sons of Confederate Veterans, Southern Station, Box 5164, Hattiesburg, MS 39401.
The Union and Confederate organizations mentioned in this and the previous paragraph, along with several others, are listed in:
__M. Fish, editor, ENCYCLOPEDIA OF ASSOCIATIONS, Gale Research Co., Detroit, MI, latest issue.

Instructions for seeking records of these societies have been given in section 3 of Chapter 5. Inquiries may also be addressed (with an SASE) to the above addresses. The retired records of the national GAR may be inquired about by writing:
__Library of Congress, Washington, DC 20540.

6. Photographs and prints

In 1822 J. N. Niepce produced the first photograph, but it was not until somewhat later that the technique lost some of its cumbersomeness and began to be semi-portable and thus fairly widespread. Fortunately this had occurred before the Civil War, permitting Matthew B. Brady and others to make many photographs of Civil War events. Numerous collections have been made but the best ones are:
__F. T. Miller, THE PHOTOGRAPHIC HISTORY OF THE CIVIL WAR, Yoseloff, New York, NY (reprint 1957), 10 volumes in 5.
__M. B. Brady, COLLECTION OF CIVIL WAR PHOTOGRAPHS, National Archives, Washington, DC, 1958, 4 reels of microfilm.
Among the better one-volume works are:
__D. H. Donald, DIVIDED WE FOUGHT, Macmillan, New York, NY, 1953.
__H. W. Elson, THE CIVIL WAR THROUGH THE CAMERA, Trow, New York, NY, 1912.
__J. B. Egan and A. W. Desmond, THE CIVIL WAR: ITS

PHOTOGRAPHIC HISTORY, Character, Wellesley Hills, MA, 1941.
__H. D. Milhollen, BEST PHOTOS OF THE CIVIL WAR, Arco, New York, NY, 1961.
Many of the coffee-table books and histories mentioned in section 5 of Chapter 1 also contain photographs.

In addition to photographers, artists also accompanied troops in their military activities. This has led to a sizable number of drawings, sketches, illustrations, and pictures. However, one must exercise a degree of caution, because many of them are quite inaccurate on what they portray, indicating that an abundance of material was produced out of the imaginations of artists and not from first-hand observation. Among the better art books are the following:
__R. M. Ketchum, THE AMERICAN HERITAGE PICTORIAL HISTORY OF THE CIVIL WAR, American Heritage, New York, NY, 1960.
__S. W. Sears, THE AMERICAN HERITAGE CENTURY COLLECTION OF CIVIL WAR ART, American Heritage, New York, NY, 1974.
__E. Forbes, A CIVIL WAR ARTIST AT THE FRONT, Oxford, New York, NY, 1957.
__L. Kurz and A. Allison, engravers, BATTLES OF THE CIVIL WAR, Pioneer Press, Little Rock, AR, 1960.
__H. W. Williams, THE CIVIL WAR: THE ARTISTS' RECORD, Corcoran Gallery, Washington, DC, 1961.
__F. Leslie, ILLUSTRATED HISTORY OF THE CIVIL WAR, Fairfax Press, New York, NY, 1895 (reprint 1977).
Again many of the coffee-table books and histories mentioned in section 5 of Chapter 1 also contain pictures. Numerous other books containing photographs and pictures of the Civil War are listed in:
__A. Nevins, J. I. Robertson, and B. I. Wiley, editors, CIVIL WAR BOOKS: A CRITICAL BIBLIOGRAPHY, LA State Press, Baton Rouge, LA, 1967-9, 2 volumes.

7. Personal book collection

If it turns out to be your intent to extend your research to the Civil War military careers of your 4 great-grandfathers and their brothers plus the brothers of your 4 great-grandmothers (or even to your 8 great-great-grandfathers and their brothers plus the brothers of your 8 great-great-grandmothers, depending on your age), it is recommended that you build up a core library of Civil War volumes to facilitate your work. Listed below are the books which would save you much travel to libraries:

__(a) G. B. Everton, Sr., HANDY BOOK FOR GENEALOGISTS, Everton Publishers, Logan, UT, 1981.

__(b) Geo. K. Schweitzer, GENEALOGICAL SOURCE HANDBOOK, $8 postpaid from the author at the address on the title page of this book.

__(c) J. C. Neagles, CONFEDERATE RESEARCH SOURCES, Ancestry Publishing, Salt Lake City, UT, 1986.

__(d) R. M. Ketchum, THE AMERICAN HERITAGE PICTORIAL HISTORY OF THE CIVIL WAR, American Heritage, New York, NY, 1960.

__(e) B. Catton, THE CENTENNIAL HISTORY OF THE CIVIL WAR, Doubleday, Garden City, NY, 1965, 3 volumes.

__(f) C. E. Dornbusch, MILITARY BIBLIOGRAPHY OF THE CIVIL WAR, NY Public Library, New York, NY, 1961-72, 3 volumes.

__(g) H. H. Kagen, THE AMERICAN HERITAGE PICTORIAL ATLAS OF US HISTORY, American Heritage, New York, NY, 1966.

__(h) A. H. Cromie, A TOUR GUIDE TO THE CIVIL WAR, Dutton, New York, NY, 1975.

__(i) K. W. Munden and H. P. Beers, GUIDE TO FEDERAL ARCHIVES RELATING TO THE CIVIL WAR, National Archives Publication No. 63-1, General Services Administration, Washington, DC, 1963.

__(j) H. P. Beers, GUIDE TO THE ARCHIVES OF THE GOVERN-MENT OF THE CONFEDERATE STATES OF AMERICA, National Archives Publication No. 68-15, General Services Administration, Washington, DC, 1968.

Book (a) is a basic genealogical tool listing all the counties in the US, their county seats, their county seat addresses, their records officials, their vital records holdings, plus abundant general genealogical record data for each state. Book (b) is a practical guidebook to genealogical research listing all major plus many minor genealogical information sources with precise details and exact instructions for obtaining the information. Book (c) goes into great detail concerning records in the archives of the Confederate states. Book (d) is an excellent illustrated one-volume history of the Civil War which will give you a broad overview of the sequence of events that will permit you to place your Civil War ancestor in the stream of occurrences. Books

(e) will provide you further information on specific battles and campaigns in which your ancestor was involved. Books (f) are the three-volumed keys to detailed historical accounts of regiments which permit you to follow your ancestor's day-to-day military career. Book (g) is notable because it provides you with detailed maps of major battles so that you can trace the action of your ancestor's regiment precisely as the battles progressed. Book (h) is an exceptional volume. It gives summary military histories of each state, summary histories of museums, buildings, memorials, statues, and markers so that you can become acquainted with exactly what remains from Civil War times in the places your ancestor served his military duty. Books (i) and (j) are the detailed listings of the vast Civil War records available to you in the National Archives. Many of these records have scarcely been touched by genealogical researchers.

8. Books and bookshops

Most volumes on the Civil War which are in print are available from any standard bookstore who will be willing to order for you. They will usually have a copy of the basic reference work which lists most in-print books:
    BOOKS IN PRINT, Author, Title, & Subject Guides, Bowker, New York, NY, latest issue, 6 volumes.
If, therefore, you want to purchase a certain book on the Civil War, you should first find out if the book is in print by consulting the above reference volume at your bookstore or in a library. There are three other works that can be quite helpful to you for locating books. The first of these lists older books which have been reprinted. There are many such books in both the genealogical and the Civil War fields. This work is:
    GUIDE TO REPRINTS and SUBJECT GUIDE TO REPRINTS, Guide to Reprints, Kent, CT, latest issue, 4 volumes.
The second is an extensive listing of books and documents which has been made available on microfilm. This list is to be found in:
    GUIDE TO MICROFORMS IN PRINT, Subject, Author, and Title Listings, Microform Review, Westport, CT, latest issue, 2 volumes.
The third reference work is a listing of rare books which a company will photocopy for you. This volume is entitled:

__BOOKS ON DEMAND, Author, Subject, and Title Guides,
University Microfilms, Ann Arbor, MI, latest issue, 3
volumes.
All the above listings should be consulted as you seek to
purchase books relating to your ancestor and his Civil
War activities.

When you want to purchase Civil War books, you will
find that your needs can be courteously and efficiently
met if you deal with one of the many bookstores which
specialize in Civil War volumes. They usually have all
the reference volumes discussed in the previous paragraph, and they will use them in seeking to find a book
you ask them for. However, where these specialty bookstores really can be indispensible are for cases in which
you need to purchase an out-of-print book. They maintain
an information network which permits them to make nation-
wide searches for such volumes. Civil War specialty
bookstores will be found in the following directory:
__AMERICAN BOOK TRADE DIRECTORY, Bowker, New York, NY,
latest edition.
Look under the state and cities near you and take particular note of bookstores described as antiquarian. Then
check the detailed listing to see if the antiquarian
bookstores you have located specialize in Civil War,
American History, 19th Century, Military, Confederate, or
other pertinent book categories.

Very sizable listings of Civil War books (many out
of print) have been published. These list over 10,000
volumes including general works, regimental histories,
and Confederate imprints.
__T. Broadfoot, CIVIL WAR BOOKS, A PRICED CHECKLIST,
Broadfoot's Bookmark, Wilmington, NC, latest edition.
__A. Nevins, J. I. Robertson, Jr., and B. I. Wiley, CIVIL
WAR BOOKS, A CRITICAL BIBLIOGRAPHY, LA State University
Press, Baton Rouge, LA, 1967.
__C. E. Dornbusch, MILITARY BIBLIOGRAPHY OF THE CIVIL
WAR, NY Public Library, New York, NY, 1961-72, 3
volumes.
__M. Mullins and R. Reed, THE UNION BOOKSHELF, A SELECTED
CIVIL WAR BIBLIOGRAPHY, Broadfoot's Bookmark, Wilming-
ton, NC, 1982.
If you are searching for details relating to your Civil
War veteran's military unit, these listings should be
consulted.

Six times a year a very valuable journal dealing with selling, buying, and trading of Civil War books, photographs, and relics is published. Every person interested in Civil War research in detail should subscribe to this useful publication:
CIVIL WAR BOOK EXCHANGE, PO Box 15432, Philadelphia, PA 19149.

Address delivered at the dedication of the cemetery at Gettysburg.

Four score and seven years ago our fathers brought forth on this continent, a new nation, conceived in Liberty, and dedicated to the proposition that all men are created equal.

Now we are engaged in a great civil war, testing whether that nation, or any nation so conceived and so dedicated, can long endure. We are met on a great battle field of that war. We have come to dedicate a portion of that field, as a final resting place for those who here gave their lives that that nation might live. It is altogether fitting and proper that we should do this.

But, in a larger sense, we can not dedicate — we can not consecrate — we can not hallow — this ground. The brave men, living and dead, who struggled here have consecrated it, far above our poor power to add or detract. The world will little note, nor long remember what we say here, but it can never forget what they did here. It is for us the living, rather, to be dedicated here to the unfinished work which they who fought here have thus far so nobly advanced. It is rather for us to be here dedicated to the great task remaining before us — that from these honored dead we take increased devotion to that cause for which they gave the last full measure of devotion — that we here highly resolve that these dead shall not have died in vain — that this nation, under God, shall have a new birth of freedom — and that government of the people, by the people, for the people, shall not perish from the earth.

Abraham Lincoln.

November 19, 1863.

Books by George K. Schweitzer

CIVIL WAR GENEALOGY. A 78-paged book of 316 sources for tracing your Civil War ancestor. Chapters include I: The Civil War, II: The Archives, III: National Publications, IV: State Publications, V: Local Sources, VI: Military Unit Histories, VII: Civil War Events.

GENEALOGICAL SOURCE HANDBOOK. A 100-paged book describing all major and many minor sources of genealogical information with precise and detailed instructions for obtaining data from them.

GEORGIA GENEALOGICAL RESEARCH. A 235-paged book containing 1303 sources for tracing your GA ancestor along with detailed instructions. Chapters include I: GA Background, II: Types of Records, III: Record Locations, IV: Research Procedure and County Listings (detailed listing of records available for each of the 159 GA counties).

KENTUCKY GENEALOGICAL RESEARCH. A 154-paged book containing 1191 sources for tracing your KY ancestor along with detailed instructions. Chapters include I: KY Background, II: Types of Records, III: Record Locations, IV: Research Procedure and County Listings (detailed listing of records available for each of the 120 KY counties).

NEW YORK GENEALOGICAL RESEARCH. A 240-paged book containing 1426 sources for tracing your NY ancestor along with detailed instructions. Chapters include I: NY Background, II: Types of Records, III: Record Locations, IV: Research Procedure and NY City Record Listings (detailed listing of records available for the 5 counties of NY City), V: Record Listings for Other Counties (detailed listing of records available for each of the other 57 NY counties).

NORTH CAROLINA GENEALOGICAL RESEARCH. A 190-paged book containing 1233 sources for tracing your NC ancestor along with detailed instructions. Chapters include I: NC Background, II: Types of Records, III: Record Locations, IV: Research Procedure and County Listings (detailed listing of records available for each of the 100 NC counties).

PENNSYLVANIA GENEALOGICAL RESEARCH. A 225-paged book containing 1309 sources for tracing your PA ancestor along with detailed instructions. Chapters include I: PA Background, II: Types of Records, III: Record Locations, IV: Research Procedure and County Listings (detailed listing of records available for each of the 67 PA counties).

REVOLUTIONARY WAR GENEALOGY. A 110-paged book containing 407 sources for tracing your Revolutionary War ancestor. Chapters include I: Revolutionary War History, II: The Archives, III: National Publications, IV: State Publications, V: Local Sources, VI: Military Unit Histories, VII: Sites and Museums.

SOUTH CAROLINA GENEALOGICAL RESEARCH. A 190-paged book containing 1107 sources for tracing your SC ancestor along with detailed instructions. Chapters include I: SC Background, II: Types of Records, III: Record Locations, IV: Research Procedure and County Listings (detailed listing of records available for each of the 47 SC counties and districts).

TENNESSEE GENEALOGICAL RESEARCH. A 136-paged book containing 1073 sources for tracing your TN ancestor along with detailed instructions. Chapters include I: TN Background, II: Types of Records, III: Record Locations, IV: Research Procedure and County Listings (detailed listing of records available for each of the 96 TN counties).